According to the Book

Using TIMSS to investigate the translation of policy into practice through the world of textbooks

by

Gilbert A. Valverde

*University at Albany,
State University of New York*

Leonard J. Bianchi

*Flint Public Schools,
Michigan*

Richard G. Wolfe

*Ontario Institute for Studies in Education,
University of Toronto*

William H. Schmidt

Michigan State University

and

Richard T. Houang

Michigan State University

KLUWER ACADEMIC PUBLISHERS

DORDRECHT / BOSTON / LONDON

A C.I.P. Catalogue record for this book is available from the Library of Congress.

ISBN 1-4020-1033-8 (HB)
ISBN 1-4020-1034-6 (PB)

Published by Kluwer Academic Publishers,
P.O. Box 17, 3300 AA Dordrecht, The Netherlands.

Sold and distributed in North, Central and South America
by Kluwer Academic Publishers,
101 Philip Drive, Norwell, MA 02061, U.S.A.

In all other countries, sold and distributed
by Kluwer Academic Publishers,
P.O. Box 322, 3300 AH Dordrecht, The Netherlands.

Printed on acid-free paper

Printed in the Netherlands.

Table of Contents

Preface

Curriculum frameworks or content standards acquired special prominence in educational policy in the latter half of the twentieth century – a prominence still evident as we enter the twenty-first. Many of the world's educational systems have experienced an important shift of focus in education policies during this period. The stress had traditionally fallen on improving material investments and guaranteeing universal access to public education. The 1980s and 1990s, however, brought a stronger emphasis on the conceptual understandings, procedural knowledge and other academic objectives to be met by all students in primary and secondary education – and thus a renewed interest in the intended curriculum as one of the most critical components of educational policy. The movement towards the development or reform of educational content standards in many educational systems reflects this emphasis on the quality of the content of the intended curriculum. Policy makers and educational leaders have favored the development of official curricula and a variety of implementation tools to insure the delivery and attainment of socially significant disciplinary content. Most new curricula stipulate the acquisition of higher order knowledge by all students, and such prescription tends to be informed by the type and amount of knowledge that is perceived to be critical for students to function effectively in society and in the economy.

A considerable body of work has been contributed to support the use of educational policy programs focused on the quality of the content of schooling in what has been termed content-driven reform. It is stated that ambitious curriculum intentions must be formulated and subsequently appropriate mechanisms must be designed to implement these curricula so that students may have the opportunity to attain high levels of achievement. Content-driven reform holds that a core specification of curriculum goals provides the basis for setting up a policy structure designed to enhance the achievement of pupils. Thus, the intended curriculum is projected to directly impact teacher training and certification, school course offerings, instructional resources, and systems of accountability.

Paradoxically, the specification of 'curricula for high achievement' and the attendant policy instruments that might be concerned with translating these into 'high achievement' opportunities to learn in the classroom have not greatly benefited from empirical work – cross-national or otherwise.

Certainly high expectations concerning the role of policies regarding curriculum intentions have been held in many countries. In a survey of thirty-eight nations conducted as a part of the Third International Mathematics and Science Study (TIMSS), the majority reported a number of reforms and managed changes in the content, pedagogy and technology prescribed in national curriculum policy for school mathematics and science.

Programs of study, content standards, curriculum frameworks and the like are, however, policy instruments designed at a great distance from classrooms – they influence the classroom decisions of teachers, but often provide little in the way of detailed guidance regarding the day-to-day management of educational opportunities in classrooms.

Textbooks are commonly charged precisely with the role of translating policy into pedagogy. They represent an interpretation of policy in terms of concrete actions of teaching and learning. Textbooks are the print resources most consistently used by teachers and their students in the course of their joint work. Results from the TIMSS reports clearly depict the influence that textbooks exert on the results of that work.

This book inspects textbooks in detail, specifying how they go about the business of translating policy into pedagogy. Thus, this book belongs to the body of work from the TIMSS that seeks to explain how cross-national attainments in student achievement are related to features of educational policy and its implementation. This work continues the vision of Benjamin Bloom, Thorsten Husén and their colleagues, who inaugurated the line of research to which the authors of the current volume are heirs, with the purpose of speaking to issues of educational policy and practice. Clearly, one issue of pervading importance to the nations that participated in TIMSS was the quality of educational opportunities afforded students to learn mathematics and science – and the instruments that optimize such quality.

Acknowledgements

The authors are indebted to the early leaders of the International Association for the Evaluation of Educational Achievement (IEA) for creating the institution under the auspices of which this research was conducted. We are also beholden to the national research coordinators of the TIMSS participating countries who led this work in their nations and shouldered a great deal of the logistic burden. But most especially, we are grateful to the coders in each country – many of whom were classroom teachers – who made it possible to collect data from 630 mathematics and science textbooks from around the world. This book, and the many other findings and insights derived from the TIMSS Curriculum Analysis, are a tribute to their effort.

We also acknowledge three of our graduate students, Virginia Keen who tirelessly managed quality control and a myriad of other tasks essential for guaranteeing the best possible curriculum analysis data set, and Christine DeMars and Shelley Naud, 'for their unrelenting efforts in carrying out the analyses that supported this book. We further acknowledge Jacqueline Babcock and JaNice Benjamin for their help in managing the project.

The work presented in this book was funded by the National Science Foundation (NSF) through two grants (RED 9252935 and REC 9550107) and we gratefully acknowledge this support. However, the authors alone assume responsibility for the results and interpretation presented here.

To the memories of

Benjamin S. Bloom

and

Leigh Burstein

Pioneers and champions of cross-national educational research.

Chapter 1

Textbooks and Educational Opportunity

"Ability is nothing without opportunity."
Napoleon I

Attending school dominates the lives of most children around the world. Much evidence indicates that their specific schooling experiences vary considerably from country to country. There is evidence that they even vary among schools and among classrooms in the same country. However, within this variety there are parts of the school setting so common as to be virtually universal. Textbooks are one such element. Perhaps only students and teachers themselves are a more ubiquitous element of schooling than textbooks. As such a central facet of schooling, understanding textbooks is essential to understanding the learning opportunities provided in educational systems around the world.

Textbooks help define school subjects as students experience them. They represent school disciplines to students. They translate a country's curriculum policies into such representations. These representations are stories their authors and editors intend to be told in classrooms over the time that the books are used – often a full school year or grade. They are a fixed component providing an unchanging reference to the nature of these school subjects for teachers, students, and their parents.

Schooling is a dynamic activity and textbooks function within this dynamic structure of schooling. They are one in a series of resources that educational systems assemble to provide children opportunities to be exposed to and master knowledge and skills deemed important by their societies. These resources are organized purposively. Educational systems presumably are concerned with organizing such resources into optimal structures that create the best opportunities for children to learn.

Textbooks themselves are unchanging at a given point in schooling. However, they are flexible as tools used by school systems, schools, teachers and students. Teachers and students use them in varied ways. However, they are written to set down a particular vision of school subjects and reflect the intention of the authors. Thus, when they open their school texts, students and teachers access distinctive conceptions of what school subjects are. They look through a "glass" designed to reveal a particular vision. Teachers and students inevitably modify this vision as a result of using this tool in the classroom setting. However, some modifications are more likely than others, given the invariant nature of the text and the roles it plays in promoting pedagogical strategies. Hence, textbooks exert probabilistic influences on the educational opportunities that take place in the classrooms in which they are used.

Textbooks are artifacts. They are a part of schooling that many stakeholders have the chance to examine and understand (or misunderstand). In most classrooms they are the physical tools most intimately connected to teaching and learning. Textbooks are designed to translate the abstractions of curriculum policy into operations that teachers and students can carry out. They are intended as mediators between the intentions of the designers of curriculum policy and the teachers that provide instruction in classrooms. Their precise mediating role may vary according to the specifics of different nations, educational systems, schools and classrooms. Their great importance is constant.

They mediate between the intent of curricular policy and the instruction that occurs in classrooms. This suggests that textbooks have a strong impact on what occurs in classrooms. Textbooks' substantial impact on teacher's instructional decision-making has been extensively documented in studies in a number of countries.[1]

Educational priorities are often central issues politically contested. Since textbooks embody such priorities, they acquire a relevance that is not only pedagogical but profoundly political as well. Textbooks define school subjects not only for teachers and pupils, but for the public as well. They are thus closely scrutinized in the context of debates on directions in education. They are central features of the structure of schooling's educational opportunities. Consequently, and ultimately, they affect the life chances of students.

Textbooks are intimately related to classroom instruction. As such they are close to teachers, pupils and their families. As a result their content and structure are extremely important – and visible – in the politics of schooling. It is increasingly obvious that they serve important political purposes, helping to configure the environment in which schooling occurs.

In school systems across the world, textbooks' contents have been important promoters of specific visions of schooling. They are thus central characters in the politics of education. They have played part in national-level ideological upheavals such as the Cultural Revolution in the People's Republic of China,[2] and in intensive interest-group competition in the context of educational reforms in France,[3] Taiwan[4] and the Netherlands.[5]

In periods of perceived educational crisis, school systems and the educational opportunities they make available are under the critical scrutiny of key social actors. It is then that the content of textbooks is most likely to be the subject of political controversy. Certainly, this seems to be illustrated in the case of the United States. Textbooks – and the vision of school mathematics and science that they manifest – have become the center of attention as school districts attempt to change textbooks in the face of concerted public opposition.[6] State textbook adoption agencies and independent monitoring groups find that the textbook market does not offer options that satisfy their conception of quality.[7] School districts and states find it necessary to include disclaimers in school biology textbooks to defuse politically contentious issues between scientific and religious conceptions of how living organisms have acquired the morphological and physiological characteristics that distinguish them.[8]

TIMSS AND THE ANALYSIS OF TEXTBOOKS

In 1991 a group of researchers from six nations under the name of the Survey of Mathematics and Science Opportunities (SMSO) began work to develop the Third International Mathematics and Science Study (TIMSS) to be conducted by the International Association for the Evaluation of Educational Achievement (IEA).[9] TIMSS became the largest twentieth century cross-national research study in education. Following up previous IEA studies focusing separately on mathematics and science education, the IEA initially intended the TIMSS to study two student populations: nine and thirteen-year-olds. However, the decision was made to make this study a coordinated investigation of both school science and mathematics – a decision in which the political salience of both mathematics and science education on the international scene played a substantial role. This led to a decision to include a third student population as well. These were students in the final year of secondary school in each of the participating nations. In TIMSS these populations became known as Populations 1, 2 and 3 – corresponding respectively to students of nine-years and thirteen-years of age and students in the final year of secondary school.[10] When the TIMSS was finally conducted more than half a million students from forty countries were tested. A comprehensive effort was made to characterize the opportunities for mathematical and scientific learning that each of the participating countries provided for students in the TIMSS focal populations.

As part of its characterization of school science and mathematics across many countries, the SMSO designed the most comprehensive cross-national study of textbooks ever attempted. This unprecedented effort resulted from the development of a model of educational opportunities intended to guide development of all TIMSS data collection instruments and analytical methods. Within this model textbooks play a key role in mediating between systemic intentions and classroom instruction.

The TIMSS was designed to be a study of educational systems as they exist to deliver educational experiences to students.[11] As such, a complex array of interrelated data collections was conceived. Within this, the data on textbooks were an important component. These data collections were interrelated through a systemic model of educational opportunities.

A MODEL OF EDUCATIONAL OPPORTUNITIES

The starting point for the model of educational opportunities in school mathematics and science is a tripartite model of curriculum. It has been a traditional feature of studies conducted under the auspices of the International Association for the Evaluation of Educational Achievement (IEA)[12] for some time.[13] This model (Exhibit 1.1) makes an analytical distinction between curriculum as system goals, curriculum as instruction, and curriculum as student achievement. These dimensions are known, respectively, as the intended, implemented, and attained curriculum.

Exhibit 1.1   The IEA Tripartite Curriculum Model

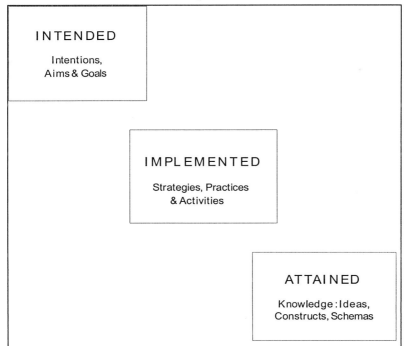

INTENDED
Intentions,
Aims & Goals

IMPLEMENTED
Strategies, Practices
& Activities

ATTAINED
Knowledge: Ideas,
Constructs, Schemas

A systemic model of educational opportunity was developed.[14] The model centers on the notion that one purpose of an educational system, and a primary focus of its pedagogical role, is to create opportunities for students to learn school subjects.

We understand *educational opportunity* to mean the configuration of social, political and pedagogical conditions to provide pupils chances to acquire knowledge, to develop skills and to form attitudes concerning school subjects. The concept of educational opportunity used in our model is a direct heir to classical insights regarding "Opportunity to Learn" derived from earlier studies conducted by the IEA.[15] These have been extended in both the areas of educational measurement,[16] and educational policy studies.[17]

This model parallels other scholarship on education that has inquired into determinants of academic achievement and attainment using models of classroom processes and their relationship to student outcomes and the organization of schooling. There are, for example important correspondences between our model and classical and contemporary ideas from the sociology of education regarding schooling as a process in which both teachers and students are primary actors conditioned by the social organization of school systems, schools and classrooms.[18] Our model is also largely congruent with many insights from microeconomic research that has uncovered the effect on student achievement of teachers' decisions regarding the allocation of instructional resources within classrooms.[19]

Our model focuses on the relationships between both the intention and implementation levels of educational policy making. The model envisions social, political and pedagogical conditions for teaching and learning as structures in which the goals and actions of a variety of institutional and individual actors are interrelated. These structures include especially important political and pedagogical components, particularly regarding the establishment of goals for education. In this schema we recognize curricula, textbooks, schools, and teachers as elements that both define and delimit the possible experiences afforded to students for learning mathematics and the sciences. We argue that the opportunity structures present in various school systems influence the actual accomplishments of students in schools.

Exhibit 1.2 depicts the constructs and interrelationships in the model. The columns represent the four primary research questions of TIMSS, and the four rows specify the four levels of the educational system that were examined. The arrows show the network of relationships among the constructs.

The study of textbooks is a central component of the TIMSS research design as can be appreciated from this model. The study of textbooks provides key indicators in the characterization of opportunity in the 48 nations that participated in this part of the study. The model states that the intended curriculum sets parameters that emphasize certain potential learning experiences and constrain others. The intended curriculum is viewed as formulated by the nation or at some sub-national (i.e., provincial, municipal, district, etc.) level, by specifying learning goals.

Exhibit 1.2 The SMSO Model

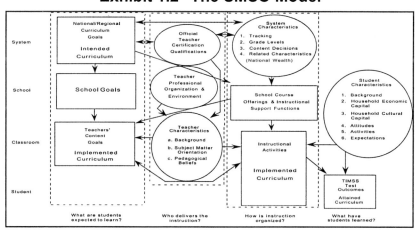

The model postulates a relationship between intention and instructional practice in which the inclusion of a learning goal in the intended curriculum does not guarantee that it will be covered. Including an intention as a goal does not guarantee that the opportunity to attain that goal will actually be provided in classrooms – but does greatly increase the probability that it will. The absence of a goal similarly increases the probability that potential learning experiences related to that goal will not be provided. However, as before, we deal only with differences in probabilities – in the probability distributions of potential learning experiences – and not with certainty that an opportunity will not be delivered. Educational systems build structures of educational opportunity using a variety of instruments. Each of these instruments plays a distinctive role in conveying educational goals and influencing their pursuit in classrooms.

The model envisions content standards, frameworks, programs of study and the like as primary defining elements of potential educational experiences. They help shape goals and expectations for learning. These visions intended to guide experiences are themselves important features of an educational system. They are features of educational policy and are tied to attendant social and political conceptions of educational quality. Characterizing these conceptions gauges the array of visions that are intended to guide educational systems, and provides a fundamental element in understanding the context within which curricula are implemented.

Even so, another characterization is essential for the model. This is a portrayal of the most important instruments intended to translate these goals into prescriptions or suggestions for specific opportunities to be created in classrooms. Thus, an additional important component of the TIMSS measurement strategy included a look at how textbooks provide templates for student actions in the classroom.

Accordingly, characterizing textbooks has an importance analogous role to characterizing student achievement; it is still another indicator. How textbooks are related to the intended curriculum and the particular vision that they promote regarding what students are expected to learn are among the fundamental features of educational systems. These features are central in understanding the educational experiences afforded to children in the TIMSS countries. The ability to link these features to other outcomes – such as instructional practices and student achievement – is another strength of this approach. It lets us study how potential educational experiences become transformed and actualized as curriculum is implemented in schools and classrooms.[20]

Policy makers, curriculum developers, and educators in many countries struggle with the reform of their curricula. For example, what should a "world-class curriculum", in mathematics and the sciences have as its content and as its expectations for what students should be able to do? Should it include non-cognitive goals? What policies need to be associated with such a curriculum? What types of textbooks are best able to promote new visions in ways that help enhance the ability of teachers and students to engage in challenging and meaningful pedagogical activities? If policy makers are serious in wanting to address these issues[21] as they undertake reform, then comprehensive and empirical descriptions of what different countries are actually doing are necessary as a beginning.

TEXTBOOKS AS MEDIATORS BETWEEN INTENTION AND IMPLEMENTATION

Within our conceptual framework, textbooks play a key role – they are the mediators between *intention* and *implementation*. Curriculum policy makers make decisions regarding instructional goals. These are shaped into instruments such as content standards, curriculum guides, frameworks, or other such documents. Unfortunately, these documents rarely spell out the operations that must take place to build instructional activities that embody the content present in the standards. However, textbooks are written to serve teachers and students in this way – to work on their behalf as the links between the ideas present in the intended curriculum and the very different world of classrooms. By proposing a series of concrete actions teachers and students can carry out to fulfill a curriculum's intentions, textbooks are not only mediators between intention and implementation, they are also components of opportunities to learn school subjects and have their own characteristic impact on instruction.

In related work reported elsewhere[22], statistically significant relationships have been found between textbooks and classroom instruction. This is true both in terms of the percentage of a country's teachers who cover topics promoted in textbooks and also in terms of the average proportion of instructional time devoted to each topic. This relationship held true for most countries in both mathematics and science. Additionally, this work established significant relationships between content standards and textbooks – a finding that further supports our argument regarding the textbook's role as intermediary.[23]

The mediating role of textbooks is complex because teachers and students are not passive in creating educational opportunities. Each has a unique impact on what transpires in classrooms. Teachers and students also have visions and goals that enter into the multifaceted structure of actors, institutions, and policy instruments that together create the educational opportunities found in school systems.

The consistency and compatibility of the visions and goals of textbooks with those of curriculum policy makers, teachers and others certainly varies from country to country. This has been born out from a number of previous findings from TIMSS.[24] However, whether through the explicit directives of curriculum policy or through the forces of the market place, textbooks generally reflect curricular intention. In particular, textbooks largely reflect the content and student performance expectations present in content standards. However, this is not done consistently across all TIMSS countries, as can be seen in Exhibit 1.3.[25]

Exhibit 1.3   Consistency of Content Standards and Textbooks for a Select Set of Topics and Countries

Mathematics Topics	Australia	Austria	Canada	Czech Republic	France	Greece	Hong Kong	Japan	Netherlands	Russian Federation	Singapore	Spain	USA
Numbers													
Whole Number													
Meaning	⊕		⊕	⊕	⊕	○	⊕				+	⊕	⊕
Operations	⊕	⊕	⊕	+	⊕	⊕	⊕		⊕		+	+	⊕
Properties of Operations	⊕	+	⊕	+	⊕	⊕	⊕				+	+	⊕
Fractions & Decimals													
Common Fractions	⊕	+	⊕	+	+	+	⊕		+		+	+	⊕
Decimal Fractions	⊕	+	⊕	+	⊕	+	⊕		+		+	⊕	⊕
Relationships of Common & Decimal Fract	+	+	⊕	+	+	+	⊕		⊕		+	+	⊕
Percentages	+	⊕	⊕	+	⊕		⊕		+		⊕	+	⊕
Properties of Common & Decimal Fraction	+	+	⊕	+	+		⊕					+	⊕
Integer, Rational & Real Numbers													
Integers & Their Properties	⊕	⊕	⊕	+	⊕	+	○		⊕			⊕	⊕
Rational Numbers & Their Properties	+	○	⊕	+	⊕	+	○		⊕	⊕		⊕	⊕
Real Numbers, Their Subsets & Properties	+	⊕	⊕	+	⊕	⊕	○		+	⊕		+	⊕
Other Numbers & Number Concepts													
Binary Arithmetic and/or Other Number Ba	○		+			+	○	⊕				+	⊕
Exponents, Roots & Radicals	+	⊕	⊕	⊕	+	+	⊕		+	⊕	⊕	+	⊕
Complex Numbers & Their Properties					+	+	○					+	⊕
Number Theory	⊕		⊕	+		+	○		+			⊕	⊕
Counting	⊕		+			+	○						⊕
Estimation & Number Sense Concepts													
Estimating Quantity & Size	○	⊕	⊕				+	+	+	+		+	⊕
Rounding & Significant Figures	○	○	⊕	+		+	⊕	⊕	+	+	⊕		⊕
Estimating Computations	○	⊕	⊕	+		+	+	+	+	+		+	⊕
Exponents & Orders of Magnitude	⊕	○	⊕		+	+	+	⊕		+		+	○
Measurement													
Units	⊕	+	⊕	+	+	+	⊕		⊕		⊕	⊕	⊕
Perimeter, Area & Volume	⊕		⊕	⊕	⊕	+	⊕		⊕	○	⊕	○	⊕
Estimation & errors	⊕		⊕				⊕	⊕	○		⊕	○	⊕
Geometry: Position, Visualization & Shape													
1-D & 2-D Coordinate Geometry	⊕	⊕	⊕	⊕	+	+	⊕		+	⊕	⊕	+	⊕
2-D Geometry: Basics	⊕	⊕	⊕	+	⊕	+	⊕	⊕	+	+	⊕	⊕	⊕
2-D Geometry: Polygons & Circles	⊕	⊕	⊕	⊕	⊕	⊕	⊕	⊕	+	⊕	⊕	○	⊕
3-D Geometry	⊕	⊕	⊕	⊕	⊕	⊕	⊕		⊕		⊕	○	⊕
Vectors		○	⊕				○			⊕	○		⊕
Geometry: Symmetry, Congruence & Similarity													
Transformations	○	⊕	⊕	⊕	⊕	⊕	○	⊕	○	⊕	⊕	+	⊕
Congruence & Similarity		⊕	⊕	⊕	+		○	⊕	⊕	⊕	⊕	○	⊕
Constructions w. Straightedge & Compass	+	○	⊕	⊕	+	+	○		○	+	○	+	⊕
Proportionality													
Concepts	⊕	⊕	⊕	⊕	+	+	⊕		⊕	+	○	○	⊕
Problems	⊕	⊕	⊕	⊕	⊕	+	⊕		⊕		⊕	○	⊕
Slope & Trigonometry				⊕	⊕	⊕	⊕		○	⊕	⊕		⊕
Linear Interpolation & Extrapolation					⊕		○	⊕	○		○		○
Functions, Relations, & Equations													
Patterns, Relations & Functions	⊕	⊕	⊕	⊕	+	⊕	⊕	⊕	⊕	⊕	+	⊕	⊕
Equations & Formulas	⊕	⊕	⊕	⊕	⊕	⊕	⊕	⊕	⊕	⊕	⊕	⊕	⊕
Data Representation, Probability, & Statistics													
Data Representation & Analysis	⊕	⊕	⊕	+	⊕	⊕	⊕	⊕	⊕		○		⊕
Uncertainty & Probability	○		⊕				○		○			○	⊕

Legend: + - Present in Textbooks   ○ - Present in Curriculum Guides

TEXTBOOKS AS MODELS OF INSTRUCTION

Textbooks reflect content in their own way – a way that is meant to be suggestive of the *enactment* of intention. This is done through the presentation of paradigmatic lessons.

Across most TIMSS nations textbooks are made up of lessons. These lessons are units of instruction written to model valid ways to accomplish the substance of the book. This is true in terms of content to be mastered, expectations regarding what students should be able to do with content, and attitudes and dispositions regarding the subject matter. Thus, these lessons are presented as templates and supports for teacher-student interactions. These models, or paradigms, set forward a foundation upon which to build lessons combining with the qualifications and experience of teachers, and the resources and goals that children (and their families) bring to their education. Since textbooks are designed as templates for action, they are more closely linked with enacted teaching and learning activities than documents such as content standards, frameworks or programs of study. In view of this, characterizations of the pedagogical features of textbooks are especially important in understanding the nature of the provided educational opportunities in different countries.

Exhibit 1.4 modifies the IEA curriculum model previously presented to show the mediating role of textbooks. The embodiment of intentions contained in textbooks has a paradigmatic specificity for pedagogy. The generalities and ideas present in other instruments of intention are made concrete in a set of decisions concerning exemplary ways to promote learning in the classroom. Specific decisions are made in textbooks regarding the most appropriate sequencing of the content and the structuring of pedagogical situations where activities, explanations, examples, and exercises are assigned particular roles. These roles as they are presented in textbooks are fixed in terms of the unchanging physical nature of the textbook. However, they are instruments that schools and teachers

Exhibit 1.4   Textbooks and the Tripartite Model

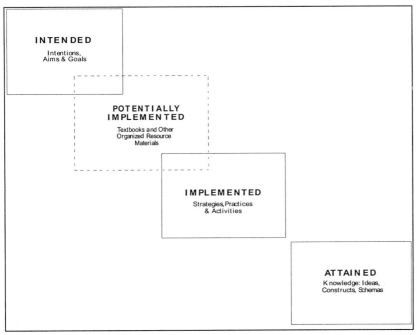

use dynamically as templates in creating educational opportunities. This dynamic use means that the precise impact of textbooks on instruction varies. Still the possible uses of these tools are finite – given the specific array of pedagogical resources that they contain by design.

CHARACTERIZING TEXTBOOKS

One question crucial to the empirical validation of the role of textbooks posited in our model of educational opportunities is whether textbooks are sufficiently variable across the TIMSS countries to play a role in explaining cross-national *differences* in educational opportunities and cross-national differences in achievement. Previous reports have documented this variability in terms of the content profiles associated with textbooks.[26] Here we are interested in whether these same textbooks vary in their form and style. We examine this variability in structure and pedagogy because we hypothesize that such characteristics are important in providing the context in which learning the content embodied in the textbook takes place. As such cross-country variability in these characteristics could be related to cross country differences in achievement. That at least is our hypothesis. Some evidence to this effect is available.[27]

Toward this end numerous measures were devised that consider a number of interrelated features of textbooks, including proposed classroom activities; amount of content covered and content complexity; the sequencing of content; physical characteristics; and the complexity of the demands for student performance. Each of these and others will be explored in detail in the following chapters.

The first type refers to the nature of the pedagogical situation posed by the textbook – whether the textbook situation is a piece of narration to be read, a set of exercises to be worked on, an example of how to solve a specified type of problem, an illustration or a graph to be examined.

The second type of measure characterizes the nature of the subject matter but not in terms of mathematics or scientific substance. Measures of the number of topics included in the book, whether the mode of presentation is abstract or concrete, are included together with a measure of the complexity associated with the topics. The latter includes whether the topic addressed is among the topics most commonly intended for students of a specific age group across the "TIMSS world."

The third type of measure deals with the sequencing of topics and includes a measure of the number of times attention to specific topics shifts from one to another. A fourth type of measure refers to the physical characteristics of textbooks – size, length, etc. Finally, the fifth textbook feature considered is a measure of the complexity of student behaviors the textbook segment is intended to elicit. For example, this might include whether students are expected to simply read and understand the material presented, to engage in problem solving or to use mathematical reasoning.

The textbooks deal with different subject matters (mathematics and science in elementary and lower secondary school, physics and college-preparatory mathematics at the end of upper secondary). They come from forty-eight educational systems around the world (some of which share cultural, linguistic or regional characteristics). They are intended for three different age groups.

Consequently, as we describe each group of measures in the following chapters, the question arises as to whether the observed population, country, and subject matter differences reflect real differences, i.e., are the characterized variations found in the data statistically significant? The subject matter differences seem logically obvious. The other questions are subtler.

We subjected a subset of variables of each of the five types of measures simultaneously to a formal analysis to gauge the statistical significance of how the measures differed by curricular area (mathematics or science), the age of the students and the country from which the textbook came. We choose twelve variables to represent the five broad areas just described. For the nature of the proposed pedagogical situation, we choose measures of the percentage of each textbook devoted to providing exercises, mathematics or science activities, worked examples or segments of narrative and related graphical material.

Content structure was represented by measures of the number of topics that account for 80 percent of the textbook space, a count of the number of times a textbook switches focus from one topic to another, and the total number of topics addressed in the book. Complexity is gauged by the extent to which the contents included in the textbook were representative of the grade-level in terms of common expectations for students across the TIMSS countries.

The number of pages represented the physical aspect of the books. Expectations regarding student behavior were represented by measures that characterize the proportion of the textbook requiring students to function at different levels of cognitive complexity. These included reading and understanding the material presented, engaging in mathematical problem solving or in scientific theorizing, and engaging in mathematical reasoning or in the investigation of the natural world.

Exhibit 1.5   Characterizing Textbook Variability

Source of Variation	Wilk's Lambda	F Value	Significance $p<$
Population	0.1518	23.23	<.0001
Region	0.0636	8.92	<.0001
Country within Region	0.0020	3.46	<.0001
Subject Matter	0.0939	143.20	<.0001
Population x Region	0.1518	2.64	<.0001
Population x Country within Region	0.0137	1.46	<.0001
Population x Subject Matter	0.3271	11.10	<.0001
Region x Subject Matter	0.2891	3.47	<.0001
Subject Matter x Country within Region	0.0094	2.49	<.0001
Population x Region x Subject Matter	0.2791	1.72	<.0001
Population x Subject Matter x Country within Region	0.0294	1.42	<.0001

We sought an initial answer to how much textbooks vary and whether such variation is systematically related to country, grade level, and subject matter differences. To answer this question we performed a multivariate analysis of variance (MANOVA).[28] The results are in Exhibit 1.5.

These analyses (based on 400 textbooks) verify that indeed textbooks exhibited statistically significant differences from each other on those 12 characteristics and that those differences were related to the subject matter of the book; the age/grade level of the student for which the books were intended; the region of the world in which the textbook was used; and the particular country within each region.[29] Using this result we do not repeat such statistical tests for each characteristic studied in chapters two through six.

The conclusion is unavoidable. Textbooks in mathematics and science are not all similar. Indeed they exhibit substantial differences in presenting and structuring pedagogical situations and these differences are systematically related to country, grade level and subject matter differences. This finding provides a fundamental backdrop for the discussion of textbooks that follows. In the chapters that follow these textbook features, and others, will be treated in depth, describing how they can be used to typify similarities and differences important in the study of textbooks.[30]

ORGANIZATION OF THE TEXTBOOK ANALYSES

Reporting on the TIMSS study of textbooks and content standards began with a detailed exploration of the mathematics and science content and expected student performances contained in these, as indicators of what students were expected to learn in the diverse school systems studied.[31] However, the role of textbooks in helping to shape the learning experiences of schoolchildren in their classrooms is more complex than establishing content goals. The relationship between textbooks, teaching, and learning is more intimate. One purpose of the current book is a fuller characterization of textbooks as pedagogical instruments in the creation of classroom opportunities to learn.

Toward that end we begin by inquiring into the "macro" structure of textbooks in order to build our understanding of how these potentially constrain the realization of the educational opportunities the textbook promotes. In this book we ignore the intellectual substance or content of those educational opportunities in our portrayal of textbooks. What that content is and how it differs across countries is extensively discussed elsewhere.[32] We deal more with the structural and pedagogical features of textbooks – those aspects that characterize form and style not substance. It is because form and style can either help or hinder the conveyance of the content themes or substance that these features of textbooks are important. At least in some ways this approach parallels formal literary analysis.

In this context Chapter two looks at indicators of the size and length of textbooks and other such physical traits. Our attention turns in Chapter 3 to how various contents are combined and sequenced within the physical structure of the book. This analysis led us to develop an identifiable textbook typology which resulted in a classification scheme based on the structure of three textbook elements – content, expectations for student performances, and the rhetorical category of the textbook element.

In Chapter 4 we turn to examining content in greater detail including measures of the number of different topics and how a book's content coverage relates to those topics that dominate "the TIMSS world" coverage at that grade level. We also examine how content is formally presented, i.e., the extent to which content is portrayed through a formally abstract system of text and symbols, or through concrete examples and real world representations. Finally, we characterize "interruptions" or "breaks" to the portrayal of content over the course of the book.

School textbooks are written to stimulate behaviors in students. The intention is not only to present information, but also to encourage the use of such information in different ways. Consequently, another important dimension of textbooks examined in Chapter 5 is the complexity of the expectations regarding what students should be able to do with the mathematics and science content.

The characterization developed in Chapters 2 through 5 we regard as description of the macro structure of textbooks. Chapter 6 examines the types of student experiences or activities that the book attempts to orchestrate for the reader. These experiences define the nature of the content exposure which students are designed to receive. The units that organize such activities are commonly called "lessons" in textbooks. We investigate how these are constructed and structured into prescriptions for pedagogical practice.

Having explored how differences and similarities exist across a number of key macro and micro features, we address in Chapter 7 whether it is possible to look beyond the immense array of differences to uncover a meaningful way to simplify it. That is, is there an identifiable and small number of clusters with common features that represent most of the books? Do these reflect grade levels? Do they reflect subject matter differences? Do they cluster by culture, tradition, or language? We conclude this book with answers to these questions. We also draw conclusions in Chapter 8 about the theoretical and empirical contributions our study makes to developing new understandings of the role of the curriculum analysis in explaining differences in textbooks, especially in terms of different educational opportunities that they make possible. We also draw policy implications from these new understandings, especially regarding the role of textbooks in curriculum-driven educational reform, returning to our guiding conception of textbooks as promoters of qualitatively distinct educational opportunities.

Notes:

[1] Ball and Feiman - Nemser 1988; Comber and Keeves 1973; Schmidt et al. 1997a; Schmidt et al. 1987; Sosniak and Perlman 1990.

[2] Kwong 1988.

[3] Hörner 1981; Magnier 1980.

[4] Chen 1997.

[5] Brenton 1982.

[6] Bingham 1998.

[7] Bridgeman and Fallon 1985; Semrad 1999.

[8] Alabama State Board of Education 1995; Roggie 1997.

[9] Schmidt et al. 1996.

[10] Relationships between ages and grade structures (especially as resulting from the age at which compulsory schooling begins in each TIMSS nation) and the desire to compare learning (change in achievement from grade to grade) led to a combined definition of the target population in the cases of elementary and lower secondary school. Thus, Population 1 was defined as the two adjacent grades in each nation in which the greatest number of nine-year-olds were enrolled. Similarly, Population 2 was defined as the two adjacent grades in each nation in which the greatest number of thirteen-year-olds were enrolled. Population 3 still refers to the single final grade of secondary schooling in each TIMSS country, regardless of mean student age. The study of textbooks was limited to the upper grade of the two in the cases of Populations 1 and 2. In the case of Population 3, the textbook study focused on the most demanding college-preparatory curriculum in Physics and Mathematics.

[11] Schmidt et al. 1996; Schmidt and McKnight 1995; Valverde 1997.

[12] The TIMSS is the most recent cross-national study of school mathematics and science conducted by the IEA, preceded by 4 prior studies in each of these content areas, conducted separately. In 1999, the TIMSS was replicated in close to 40 countries, albeit without a study of textbooks.

[13] McKnight 1979.

[14] The SMSO was a grant awarded to Michigan State University as the US Research Center for the TIMSS, which coordinated research and development work with the national research centers of a sub-group of nations participating in the TIMSS: Japan, Norway, Switzerland, Spain, France, and the US. The purpose of the SMSO was to develop the following for the TIMSS: a set of curriculum frameworks, a conceptual model to guide instrument development and data analysis, questionnaires for schools, teachers and students, techniques for measuring and studying textbooks and curriculum guides, and the specifications (blueprints) for the TIMSS achievement tests (Schmidt and Cogan 1996; Schmidt et al. 1996; Schmidt and McKnight 1995; Survey of Mathematics and Science Opportunities 1993a; Survey of Mathematics and Science Opportunities 1993b).

[15] McKnight 1979.

[16] Burstein 1993; Burstein et al. 1990; Kifer, Wolfe, and Schmidt 1992; Porter 1991; Schmidt and Burstein 1992; Schmidt and McKnight 1995.

[17] Guiton and Oakes 1995; McDonnell 1995; Porter 1993; Valverde 1997.

[18] Barr and Dreeben 1983; Bidwell, Frank, and Quiroz 1997; Bidwell and Kasarda 1980; Dreeben and Barr 1988; Dreeben and Gamoran 1986; Gamoran 1987; Gamoran and Weinstein 1998; Hallinan and Sorensen 1977; Hallinan and Sorensen 1983; Stevenson, Schiller, and Schneider 1994.

[19] Monk 1982; Monk 1984; Monk 1996; Thomas 1977; Thomas and Kemmerer 1977.

[20] A first report that relates the result of studies of such linkages is in a separate publication (Schmidt et al. 2001).

[21] The fact that slightly more nations participated in the TIMSS study of curriculum (48) than in its study of achievement (41) suggests that those nations are serious about this understanding.

[22] Schmidt et al. 2001.

[23] Final multivariate models included both textbook and content standards. As reported, the analyses uncover statistically significant interaction effects consistent with our model of educational opportunities. (See Schmidt et al. 2001).

[24] McKnight and Valverde 1999; Schmidt et al. 1996; Schmidt et al. 1999; Schmidt et al. 1997a; Schmidt et al 1997b; Schmidt et al 1997c.

[25] This table is a modified version of one originally published in Schmidt et al. 1997b.

[26] Schmidt et al. 1997b; Schmidt et al. 1997c; Schmidt et al. 2001.

[27] Schmidt et al. 2001.

[28] Multivariate analysis of variance (MANOVA) was used to test for the main and interaction effects of the design variables on the 12 dependent variables. The MANOVA used country within region, region, population and subject matter as the design variables. The 12 dependent variables were the textbook characteristics.

[29] There were also statistically significant interaction effects suggesting that textbook variability is complex.

[30] We do not, however, perform the same statistical tests for every variable we examine. The MANOVA analyses with twelve representative variables serve this purpose.

[31] Schmidt et al. 1997a; Schmidt et al. 1997b; Schmidt et al. 1997c.

[32] Schmidt et al. 2001.

Chapter 2

Physical Features of Textbooks

Textbooks around the world differ greatly in size, length, and other structural features. They also vary in the types of chapters and units they contain and in the ways they are laid out. There are also notable differences in sequencing and complexity as one examines closely the presentation of the mathematics and science topics.

There are differences in sequences and complexity specific to particular parts of textbooks designed for a small number of class periods. There are also structural features that cut across the entire book. These more pervasive features represent an important aspect of textbooks that seems likely to influence the learning opportunities the textbooks are intended to promote throughout an entire school year. We will term these more pervasive features 'macro' structures. This is in contrast to the structures associated with specific lessons intended for use in a small number of classroom instructional sessions that we term 'micro' structures.

Macro structures form the basic context in which each textbook builds up the vision of mathematics or science it intends to convey. They seem clearly to be a part of the vision of science or mathematics embodied in the textbook but also to embed or make manifest parts of that vision. In contrast, micro structures embody pedagogical intentions for a single lesson.

This chapter focuses on the physical features of textbooks. We will explore the structure of textbooks in the following chapters. We will first examine how such structures contribute to distinct types of educational opportunities throughout the entire book and then focus on how single lessons within the textbook are designed.

STUDYING THE WORLD'S TEXTBOOKS

The TIMSS curriculum analysis was designed to characterize learning opportunities in countries around the world. The textbook analysis was a part of that effort. The textbook analysis, together with teacher questionnaire data and an analysis of content standards, were used to characterize the curriculum of each participating country. This present book reports only on the textbook data.

A representative sample of textbooks was selected in each participating country. Each TIMSS country selected textbooks for analysis that represented the material to which no less then half of the mathematics and science students were exposed at each of the two grade levels studied.[1] Additionally, the textbook sample included the advanced mathematics and physics textbooks. These represented the most commonly used textbooks for the final year of college-preparatory mathematics and physics.

This resulted in a total sample of 72 mathematics and 60 science textbooks intended for nine-year-olds (fourth grade in most countries). It included 72 mathematics and 120 science textbooks intended for thirteen-year-olds (eighth grade in most countries). Finally, it included 50 advanced mathematics and 44 advanced physics textbooks intended for the final year of secondary school coursework in those subjects.[2] The TIMSS textbook study faced the challenge of characterizing these 418 mathematics and science textbooks from 48 educational systems.

The challenge of collecting valid, reliable, and comparable data across the participating countries was formidable (as was true of all other components of TIMSS). Methods had to be developed that would retain these characteristics despite the tremendous linguistic, typographic and physical variety of textbooks.

THE VARIETY OF TEXTBOOKS

To exemplify the challenge and the variety of textbooks, we consider two mathematics textbooks, one each from the People's Republic of China and from Israel. Both of these textbooks are intended for thirteen-year-old students. They are representative of the mathematics – mostly geometry – that a majority of the students in this age group are intended to master.

Exhibit 2.1   Two Geometry Textbooks
(China and Israel)

The textbook from the People's Republic of China is titled "Geometry." It is the first of two volumes published by the government-managed People's Educational Press and distributed to the students in the second grade of junior middle school (age 13). There was a teacher's manual and a student workbook that accompanied the text. The textbook itself has a length of 197 pages.

The textbook from Israel was published by the Wizeman Institute of Science, a commercial educational publisher, and is also entitled "Geometry". The book was intended for both eighth and ninth grades. The material for eighth grade is made up of pages 1 through 121. Ninth grade material is pages 123 to 224. A teacher's manual accompanied the book.[3]

School mathematics is often naively considered invariant across countries. Observers within a given country (teachers, students, educational researchers, etc.) often voice the opinion that – for example – eighth grade mathematics is pretty much the same everywhere. These observers may point out that what students achieve may differ, but (in mathematics

Exhibit 2.2   Sample Pages from Two Geometry Textbooks (China and Israel)

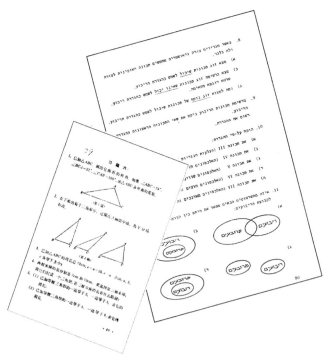

especially) the material they are expected to master is the same. Previous reports from the TIMSS have pointed out how wrong this belief is.[4] Here we will inspect these claims much more concretely and closely. Exhibit 2.2 reproduces, side-by-side a page from each of these two textbooks.

Both pages present material in two-dimensional geometry regarding polygons and/or circles. This is one of the mathematics topics most commonly intended for thirteen-year-olds to master across TIMSS countries.[5] In the case of the textbook page from the People's Republic of China, students were expected to engage in solving the problems presented. The textbook page from Israel required students to perform complex mathematical procedures, use vocabulary and notation and use elements of mathematical reasoning (justification and proof). Both are pages from geometry textbooks intended for students of the same age. Both deal with similar content. Yet the two represent different approaches to school mathematics. This kind of variability was typical across the TIMSS sampled textbooks.

A Procedure for Coding and Analyzing Textbooks

TIMSS chose to characterize textbooks as one aspect of school mathematics and science necessary to adequately portray the curriculum in each participating country. These characterizations were intended both for studying textbooks in and of themselves and for studying their relationship with student achievement in various content areas. The latter has been done and indicates the existence of both a direct and an indirect relationship between textbook content and eighth grade learning. The indirect relationship is characterized by the relationship of textbook content to the content teachers present in the classroom, which then is related to student achievement. In fact, the relationship between textbooks and teacher implementation is among the strongest found.[6]

One of the initial difficulties confronted in the coding of the textbooks was the variability in the structure and in the length of the textbooks. Therefore a necessary first step in the measurement method was to sub-divide each document into smaller units for analysis. These units would form the basis for the detailed characterization of textbooks. The most fundamental type of unit in the partitioned textbooks was labeled a "lesson." Lessons were defined in the TIMSS methodology as a segment of textbook material devoted to a single main science or mathematics topic and intended to correspond to a teacher's classroom lesson on that topic taught over one to three instructional sessions. Some textbook material (for example, reviews of previously presented topics) covered content from several lessons and units of this type were classified as "multiple-lesson pages". These two unit types, along with introductions, instructional appendices, and "other" made up the five textbook unit types used in the procedure.

Exhibit 2.3 reproduces a portion of the twenty-third unit in a Portuguese human biology textbook intended for the eighth grade. This lesson deals with the subject of the human internal environment and its regulation. It addresses a number of subtopics regarding cells and their biochemical processes, human organs and tissues and how the human body handles energy.

Dividing documents into such broad functional units simplified analysis. However, this simplification was not sufficient for measuring all the structural details needed to construct an adequate statistical characterization of the textbook. Therefore the textbook units themselves were subdivided further into smaller units called "blocks." The five boxes on the pages of the Portuguese textbook displayed in Exhibit 2.3 represent blocks. Exhibit 2.4 shows how the blocking procedure was done for the two pages reproduced from a Mexican mathematics textbook intended for thirteen-year-olds. These are the first two pages of a single lesson found in Unit 33. The unit is about solving systems of equations by the method of substitution.

Exhibit 2.3   Example of a Unit and Five Blocks from a Portuguese Science Textbook

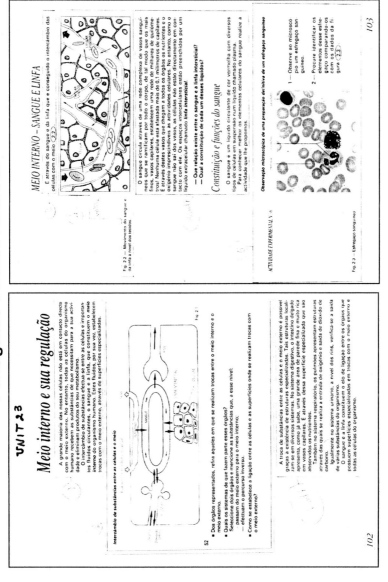

UNIT 23

Meio interno e sua regulação

A grande maioria das nossas células não está em contacto directo com o meio externo. No entanto, todas as células do organismo humano recebem as substâncias de que necessitam para a sua actividade e eliminam produtos do seu metabolismo.

O intercâmbio de substâncias efectua-se entre as células e importantes fluidos circulantes, o sangue e a linfa, que constituem o *meio interno* do organismo humano. Estes fluidos, por sua vez, estabelecem trocas com o meio externo, através de superfícies especializadas.

Intercâmbio de substâncias entre as células e o meio

Fig. 21

52

● Dos órgãos representados, refira aqueles em que se realizam trocas entre o meio interno e o meio externo.

● Quais os sistemas de que fazem parte esses órgãos?
  Seleccione dois órgãos e mencione as substâncias que, a esse nível:
   — passam do meio externo para o meio interno;
   — efectuam o percurso inverso.

● Como se estabelece a ligação entre as células e as superfícies onde se realizam trocas com o meio externo?

A troca de substâncias entre as células e o meio externo é possível graças a existência de estruturas especializadas. Tais estruturas localizam-se em diversos sistemas. No sistema digestivo, o intestino delgado apresenta, como já sabe, uma grande área de parede fina e muito rica em vasos capilares. É através dessa superfície especializada que são absorvidos os nutrientes.

Também no sistema respiratório, os pulmões apresentam estruturas através das quais se realiza a entrada de oxigénio e saída de dióxido de carbono.

Igualmente no sistema urinário, a nível dos rins, verifica-se a saída de várias substâncias do organismo.

O sangue e a linfa constituem o elo de ligação entre os órgãos que possuem superfícies especializadas em trocas com o meio externo e todas as células do organismo.

102

MEIO INTERNO – SANGUE E LINFA

É através do sangue e da linfa que e conseguido o intercâmbio das células com o meio 22.

O sangue circula através de uma rede complexa de vasos sanguíneos que se ramificam por todo o corpo, de tal modo que os mais finos, vasos capilares, estabelecem uma rede de milhares de quilómetros! Nenhuma célula está afastada mais de 0,1 milímetros de capilares. É através destes vasos que chegam a todos os órgãos os nutrientes e o oxigénio imprescindíveis às actividades celulares. No entanto, como o sangue não sai dos vasos, as células não estão directamente em contacto com ele. Os espaços intercelulares estão preenchidos por um líquido extracelular chamado *linfa intersticial*.

— Que relação existe entre o sangue e a linfa intersticial?
— Qual a constituição de cada um desses líquidos?

Fig. 2.2 — Movimento do sangue e da linfa a nível dos tecidos

Constituição e funções do sangue

O sangue e um líquido circulante de cor vermelha com diversos tipos de células em suspensão num líquido chamado plasma.
  Para conhecer melhor os elementos celulares do sangue realize a actividade que lhe propomos.

Observação microscópica de uma preparação definitiva de um esfregaço sanguíneo

ACTIVIDADE EXPERIMENTAL 6

1 — Observe ao microscópio um esfregaço sanguíneo.

2 — Procure identificar os elementos desse esfregaço comparando-os com os dados da figura 23.

Fig. 2.3 — Esfregaço sanguíneo

103

This double sub-division was codified into standardized partitioning rules that were conveyed in a series of international training sessions.[7] Each participating country had coders trained to partition their countries selected textbooks into units and blocks. The Mexican team segmented these two example pages into blocks, each with marked boundaries and numbered

Exhibit 2.4   Two Blocked Sample Textbook Pages

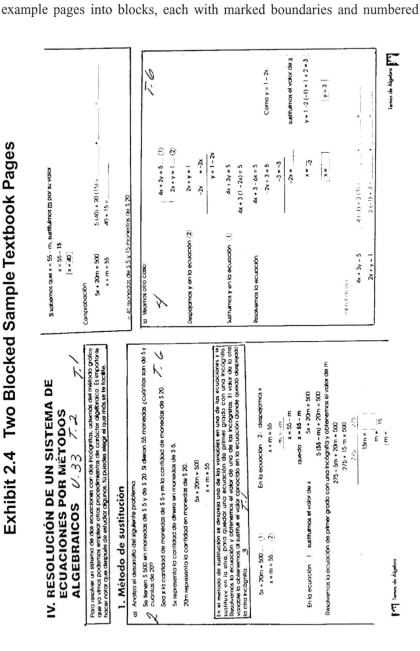

1 through 4. Each unit of every mathematics and science textbook was similarly subdivided into blocks.

By identifying different block types for textbooks, we were able to construct a more detailed characterization of each book. We used a total of ten block types in characterizing textbooks. These included narrative blocks (central, related, and unrelated instructional narrative). They also included graphic blocks (those related to narrative, those not directly related to narrative). Finally they also included exercise and question sets, suggested activities, worked examples, and "other" block types.

In the case of the example in Exhibit 2.4, four blocks were marked and numbered on the two pages.[8] (Note that Block 3 is within Block 2.) Each block was labeled with a number that indicated its type – here types 1,6, 1, and 6, respectively. Block 1 is translated roughly as "To solve a system of two equations with two unknowns, aside from the graphic method that we have just seen [in pages not shown here], we can use other procedures of an algebraic nature." Headings carry additional information – here what follows is on the "method of substitution." Headings also indicate that Block 2 ("a. Analyze the development of the following problem") and Block 4 ("b. Let's see another case.") are worked examples which the student is to study. Within the first worked example (Block 2), there is an included narrative block that begins "In the substitution method one of the variables in one of the equations is found…."

The strategy in the opening pages of this unit is clear. A general statement is made – algebraic methods and previously learned graphical methods may be used to solve systems of equations. A worked example of the method of substitution is presented. Within that example, a brief narrative segment summarizes the strategy of the method of substitution. A second worked example is presented. The first example is a contextualized problem involving currency. The second is a mathematical exercise not directly linked to anything else. The measurement procedure must reduce all of this detail to elements essential for comparing textbooks across countries. One element of the detail retained, for example, is the block type. This involves recording that the rhetorical strategy on these two pages was narrative and worked examples (block types 1 and 6).

Partitioning and indicating the types of units and blocks were central tasks in preparing textbook abstracts. The most important component of the procedure was recording the mathematical or scientific subject matter covered in the textbook. This was followed closely by recording the types of expectations concerning what students were intended to do with the subject matter contained in the textbook material as well as some notion of non-cognitive objectives if present.

To measure these curricular elements in textbooks required the development of a common category framework and descriptive language. This also allowed them to be related to measures derived from the observations and videotapes of actual lessons, achievement tests, surveys and other components of TIMSS. Any description of content had to use common terms, categories, and standardized procedures whether it was classifying a textbook block, an achievement test item, or linking a questionnaire response or observation to other parts of the TIMSS. This was done to facilitate statistical analysis.

Two framework documents – one for mathematics, the other for the sciences – provide this common language.[9] Each framework has several facets and several levels. Both consider three aspects of the subject matter (See Appendix A). The first aspect is *content*, which is the subject matter or topic addressed. The second aspect is *performance expectations*, which is what students are expected to be able to do with particular content. The third and final aspect measured with the frameworks is *perspectives*, which refer to any overarching orientation to the subject matter and its place among the disciplines and in the everyday world.[10]

Thus, after textbook units have been subdivided into blocks and these blocks assigned a type, the measurement method called for each block to be assigned as many content, performance expectation and perspective codes from the TIMSS frameworks as necessary to fully characterize it. These codes – in addition to block and unit types – form the basis of all of the analyses reported in this book.

Exhibit 2.5 demonstrates how the Mexican textbook coding team recorded the data for the two pages in our example. This figure is a reproduction of the paper coding form used by the Mexican coders to record links to document pages, block numbers, block types, and framework codes. Each column in the form refers to one textbook block. Sets of paper forms were organized by textbook unit to characterize each unit. This particular form has as its first four blocks those from the text segment reproduced in Exhibit 2.4. The first four columns represent these blocks. Block types are recorded by the numerals 1 and 6, and linked to textbook page, block number, and textbook unit.

Each of the textbook blocks received a single content code, 1.6.2 (see the Mathematics Framework in Appendix A) that corresponds to equations-related algebra. Blocks 1 and 3, the two narrative blocks, received the same performance expectation code, 2.1.3, a default code to indicate that it was simply material to be read and understood. Blocks 2 and 4, the two worked example blocks, received the same code, 2.2.2, 'performing routine procedures', indicating that this was what would be expected of the students if they had worked each example problem themselves.

Only one perspective code was used – 'using mathematics relationships in everyday life to interest students'. This is linked to the worked example of a practical problem with currency. Perspective codes were rarely found in textbooks in the TIMSS sample – and this book does not report on them. In this example, all blocks had very simple characterizations; only one block (Block 7 spanning pages 145-147) received more than one framework code in order to characterize its content.

It was common for textbook blocks to require more than one content or performance expectation code. Exhibit 2.6, for example, shows the coding of two contiguous blocks from a Japanese textbook for the science course required for population 2 students.

Exhibit 2.5 Sample Block Coding for the Two Blocked Sample Textbook Pages

COUNTRY: MEXICO

DOCUMENT ID CODE: 20 ☐ Guideline ☒ Textbook (Copy from form DA-1 or DA-4)

UNIT ID NUMBER: 33 (Copy from form DA-2) ☒ Mathematics ☐ Science

NUMBER 1 OF 2 FOR THIS UNIT.

Page no.	142	141-142	142	143	144	144	145-147	145	147-148	148
Block ID number	1	2	3	4	5	6	7	8	9	10
Block type	1	6	1	6	6	6	6	1	6	6
Content codes (1...) Primary	1.6.2	1.6.2	1.6.2	1.6.2	1.6.2	1.6.2	1.6.2	1.6.2	1.6.2	1.6.2
Secondary										
Performance expectation codes (2...) Primary	2.1.3	2.2.2	2.1.3	2.2.2	2.2.2	2.3.3	2.3.1 2.2.2	2.1.3	2.2.2	2.3.3
Secondary										
Perspective codes (3...)	∅	3.4	∅	∅	∅	3.4	∅	∅	∅	3.4

Block type codes for Curriculum Guides:
1. Official Policies
2. Objectives
3. Content element
4. Pedagogical suggestion
5. Examples
6. Assessment suggestions
7. Other

Block type codes for Textbook Materials:
1. Narrative
2. Related narrative
3. Unrelated instructional narrative
4. Related graphic
5. Unrelated graphic
6. Exercise/question set
7. Unrelated question/exercise set
8. Activity
9. Worked example
10. Other

Form completed by (Name) HILARIA MIRANDA (Title) INVESTIGADOR (Date) 30-11-9?

Here we see that the two blocks from the Japanese text are both narrative blocks.[11] Each of these blocks deals with the chemical properties of matter. In addition, Block 5 deals with the topics of 'chemical changes' (1.3.5.1) and 'atoms, ions and molecules' (1.3.2.1). Block 6 addresses all three of these topics but also presents material on 'explanations of chemical changes' (1.3.5.2).

Exhibit 2.6   Sample Block Coding for Pages from a Japanese Science Textbook

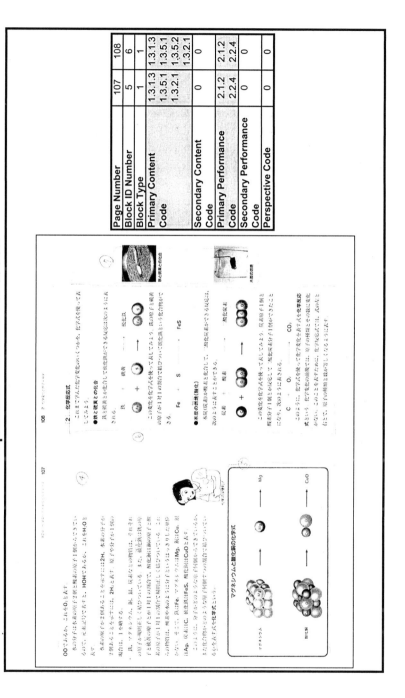

Page Number	107	108
Block ID Number	5	6
Block Type	1	1
Primary Content Code	1.3.1.3 1.3.5.1 1.3.2.1	1.3.1.3 1.3.5.1 1.3.2.1
Secondary Content Code	0	0
Primary Performance Code	2.1.2 2.2.4	2.1.2 2.2.4
Secondary Performance Code	0	0
Perspective Code	0	0

In both of these blocks, students are expected to understand complex information and engage in the construction, interpretation and application of models of scientific processes – which is indicated by the assignment of performance expectation codes 2.1.2 and 2.2.4.

In the pages that follow, we use similar characterizations of the 418 mathematics and science textbooks that were coded page-by-page using these methods. These codings are employed to construct statistical abstracts of the school mathematics and science promoted in the textbooks of over 45 countries and to examine the structure and pedagogy through which such content is conveyed.

PHYSICAL CHARACTERISTICS OF TEXTBOOKS

The most obvious aspects of the macro structure of textbooks are their physical dimensions. Within a given society the word "textbook" brings to mind a physical image that originates in the school experiences of each individual. When thinking of textbooks, many in the United States think of hefty hardbound tomes with hundreds of large pages. In Japan the word "textbook" brings to mind small, slim, paperbound volumes that are light and easily carried between home and school. Both types of textbooks are intended for use in the classroom as an important part of teaching and learning. Both represent tools intended for use over a full academic year. How textbooks differ in their physical dimensions provides us with a first global but rough indication of the possibilities and limitations in conveying the mathematics or science content they present. To put it far too simplistically, big books can contain more content but their size means it takes longer to read them and they are less likely to be covered entirely.

Pages

The number of pages is one of the most obvious physical characteristics of textbooks. Other aspects of textbooks depend on this feature. This is where we begin our exploration of the physical characteristics of textbooks.

Exhibit 2.7 depicts the percentage of textbooks in the TIMSS sample that belong to different categories based on the number of pages in the book. When we examine the number of pages across all of the documents analyzed, we find that the average number of pages for the primary grade (fourth grade) was about 125 pages for mathematics textbooks and 150 for science textbooks. For lower secondary school (eighth grade) mathematics the number of pages on average was 225. In science, the mean number of textbook pages did not vary from the primary grade textbook. Textbooks intended for mathematics specialists in their final year of secondary school averaged 375 pages, with 350 pages being the average for textbooks intended for the physics specialists.

Generally, the length of mathematics and science textbooks was quite similar on average across countries. Books for use with higher grades had more pages. The length of mathematics textbooks increased by approximately 100 pages for each of the three grade levels studied. For science textbooks, there was no such linear pattern of increase in the number of pages across grades but they did increase in size for secondary students. This is consistent with the common sense notion that, in general, at a higher grade level there is more content to learn. This additional content may be either in terms of the number of topics or in terms of the depth of coverage of topics or both, and either would likely result in more pages in the textbook.

Extreme numbers of pages were rare in the TIMSS sample, with only about 10 percent of mathematics books and 15 percent of science books having less than one hundred pages. Twelve countries had textbooks of this type, including Germany, the Russian Federation and Hong Kong. Conversely, only about 10 percent of mathematics and 5 percent of science textbooks were longer than five hundred pages in length.

Exhibit 2.7 Distribution of the Number of Pages in a Book by Subject Matter and Population

Size of Textbooks	Number of Pages	Percent of Mathematics Textbooks			Percent of Science Textbooks		
		Population 1	Population 2	Population 3	Population 1	Population 2	Population 3
Small	Less than 100	16.7	9.7	4.0	36.1	8.4	4.5
	100 to 150	31.9	9.7	4.0	29.5	25.2	4.5
	150 to 200	22.2	11.1	12.0	11.5	28.6	4.5
Medium	200 to 250	9.7	16.7	10.0	6.6	15.1	13.6
	250 to 300	6.9	15.3	16.0	8.2	10.1	11.4
	300 to 350	4.2	9.7	12.0	4.9	6.7	20.5
	350 to 400	1.4	6.9	18.0	1.6	1.7	15.9
Large	400 to 500	2.8	9.7	6.0	1.6	0.8	6.8
	500 to 600	4.2	6.9	12.0	0.0	0.8	6.8
Very Large	600 to 700	0.0	1.4	2.0	0.0	2.5	2.3
	More than 700	0.0	2.8	4.0	0.0	0.0	9.1

In mathematics, the US is certainly the exceptional case. It was the only country in the sample with virtually all of its textbooks having more than five hundred pages. Only one of the textbooks intended for nine-year-olds had fewer and it had 484 pages. In fact, the US is the only TIMSS country for which it was common to have textbooks intended for nine-year-olds with 500 pages or more. Put another way, fourth grade students in the US typically use mathematics textbooks that exceed by approximately 125 pages the average length of textbooks intended for the use of mathematics students in the last year of secondary school across the TIMSS sample of countries.

This limits the coverage of the content in US textbooks. If all of the content were to be covered, then the amount of time available for doing this would be severely limited. On the other hand, if not all content is covered then there must be some basis on which to select the content that is to be covered. This is a good example of how physical characteristics can affect the learning opportunities developed in the textbook.

By contrast, the average number of pages in a mathematics textbook that a typical nine-year-old in the "TIMSS world" is expected to cover over the school year was one-fourth the number of pages commonly expected in the US. Clearly, the challenge of 'covering' the textbook for nine-year-olds in the US is different from the challenge confronting students and teachers of the same age group in many other countries.

Other countries with histories of close ties to the English tradition had textbooks closest to the extreme length of those in the US. Those countries are Canada, New Zealand, Australia, Hong Kong, South Africa and Singapore. The only other such case is one textbook from Italy.

Science textbooks were not as long as mathematics textbooks in general. Science textbooks longer than five hundred pages came mostly from the US and Canada with an additional textbook from each of Greece,

Switzerland and Singapore – all of which were intended for advanced physics students in the final year of secondary school. The US and Canada are the only countries with textbooks intended for 13-year-olds exceeding five hundred pages. In fact, the US is the only country with science textbooks intended for 9-year-olds approaching five hundred pages in length. Some sixteen countries have science textbooks with less than one hundred pages including the People's Republic of China, Germany, Bulgaria, and Japan.

Attention to the number of pages in a textbook ignores the fact that textbook pages vary considerably in their dimensions. To adequately account for this, an additional indicator was created by multiplying the total area of pages in square centimeters by the total number of pages – to yield a number indicating the total amount of 'page surface area' per book. The results of these calculations are in Exhibit 2.8 which displays the mathematics and science distributions for each population separately (multiple textbooks from a country are all simply labeled by the country name).

Clearly total surface area increased according to the population for which the textbook was intended. This was true for both mathematics and science, where in fact the page area in textbooks intended for specialists in mathematics and physics at the end of secondary school each had an international median of 115,000 cm^2.

Extreme cases in page area are essentially the same as for the number of pages. Mathematics textbooks from Canada, Hong Kong, Australia, the United States, Singapore, and two Italian textbooks were in the highest ten percent in terms of page area – that is, textbooks with page areas in excess of 215,000 cm^2. In science, with the exception of Italy, extremely large textbooks came from the same countries that produced large mathematics textbooks – the US, Canada, Australia, Hong Kong, and Singapore.

Exhibit 2.8   Page Area of Textbooks

Mathematics Textbooks

Population 1

Country	Page Area of Textbook
Iceland	■
China	■
China	■
Iceland	■
Japan	■
Japan	■
Japan	■
Switzerlnd	■
Hong K	■
Hong K	■
Cyprus	■
Japan	■
Switzerlnd	■
Korea	■
Korea	■
Austria	■
Austria	■
Cyprus	■
Dom Rep	■
Hong K	■
Hong K	■
Argentina	■
Argentina	■
Denmark	■
Latvia	■
Switzerlnd	■
Israel	■
Czech R	■
Slovak R	■
Singapore	■
Singapore	■
Norway	■
Norway	■
Iran	■
Philippins	■
Ireland	■
Israel	■
Bulgaria	■
Israel	■
Korea	■
Korea	■
Scotland	■
Netherlnd	■

Population 1 (cont.)

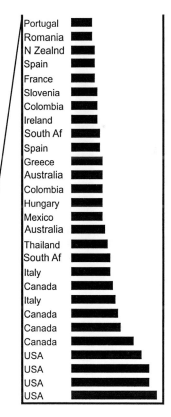

Country	Page Area of Textbook
Portugal	■
Romania	■
N Zealnd	■
Spain	■
France	■
Slovenia	■
Colombia	■
Ireland	■
South Af	■
Spain	■
Greece	■
Australia	■
Colombia	■
Hungary	■
Mexico	■
Australia	■
Thailand	■
South Af	■
Italy	■
Canada	■
Italy	■
Canada	■
Canada	■
Canada	■
USA	■
USA	■
USA	■
USA	■

Mathematics Textbooks (cont.)

Population 2

Country	Page Area of Textbook
Scotland	
Scotland	
Scotland	
Germany	
Switzerlnd	
Russian Fed	
Germany	
Bulgaria	
Romania	
Austria	
China	
China	
Romania	
Bulgaria	
Iran	
Iceland	
Netherlnd	
Slovenia	
Japan	
Czech R	
Slovak R	
Japan	
Czech R	
Slovak R	
Switzerlnd	
Netherlnd	
Russian Fed	
Dom Rep	
Israel	
Korea	
Switzerlnd	
Cyprus	
Philippins	
Tunisia	
Netherlnd	
Argentina	
Spain	
South Af	
Sweden	
Austria	
Switzerlnd	
Israel	

Population 2 (cont.)

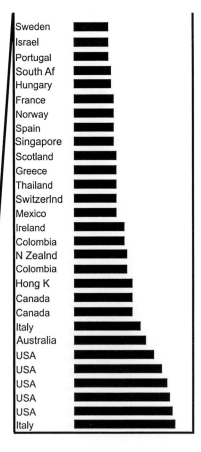

| Sweden |
| Israel |
| Portugal |
| South Af |
| Hungary |
| France |
| Norway |
| Spain |
| Singapore |
| Scotland |
| Greece |
| Thailand |
| Switzerlnd |
| Mexico |
| Ireland |
| Colombia |
| N Zealnd |
| Colombia |
| Hong K |
| Canada |
| Canada |
| Italy |
| Australia |
| USA |
| USA |
| USA |
| USA |
| USA |
| Italy |

Mathematics Textbooks (cont.)

Population 3

Country	Page Area of Textbook
Russian F	▮
Romania	▮
Romania	▮
Netherlnd	▮
Switzerlnd	▮
Switzerlnd	▮
Japan	▮
Iran	▮
Netherlnd	▮
Romania	▮
Bulgaria	▮
Iran	▮
Mexico	▮
Korea	▮
Iran	▮
Hungary	▮
Cyprus	▮
Czech R	▮
Slovak R	▮
Hong K	▮
Israel	▮
Israel	▮
South Af	▮
Greece	▮
Iceland	▮
Norway	▮
Greece	▮
N Zealnd	▮
Colombia	▮
Australia	▮
Canada	▮
N Zealnd	▮
Israel	▮
Sweden	▮
Israel	▮
Spain	▮
Colombia	▮
South Af	▮
Canada	▮
Hong K	▮
Canada	▮
Canada	▮
Australia	▮
Singapore	▮
Hong K	▮
USA	▮
USA	▮

Science Textbooks

Population 1

Country	Page Area of Textbook
Hong K	
Hong K	
Switzerlnd	
China	
China	
Hong K	
Austria	
Iceland	
Japan	
Japan	
Japan	
Hong K	
Japan	
Ireland	
Ireland	
Latvia	
Korea	
Denmark	
Bulgaria	
Austria	
Dom Rep	
Korea	
South Af	
Slovenia	

Population 1 (cont.)

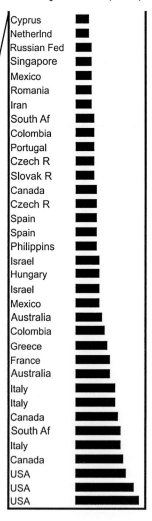

Country	Page Area of Textbook
Cyprus	
Netherlnd	
Russian Fed	
Singapore	
Mexico	
Romania	
Iran	
South Af	
Colombia	
Portugal	
Czech R	
Slovak R	
Canada	
Czech R	
Spain	
Spain	
Philippins	
Israel	
Hungary	
Israel	
Mexico	
Australia	
Colombia	
Greece	
France	
Australia	
Italy	
Italy	
Canada	
South Af	
Italy	
Canada	
USA	
USA	
USA	

Science Textbooks (cont.)

Population 2

Country	Page Area of Textbook
Iceland	▪
NetherInd	▪
Iceland	▪
Iceland	▪
Iceland	▪
China	▪
China	▪
Latvia	▪
Germany	▪
Germany	▪
NetherInd	▪
Hungary	▪
Denmark	▪
NetherInd	▪
Czech R	▪
Slovak R	▪
Romania	▪
Cyprus	▪
China	▪
Hungary	▪
Greece	▪
Denmark	▪
Czech R	▪
Slovak R	▪
Greece	▪
Bulgaria	▪
Slovenia	▪
Israel	▪
Slovenia	▪
Cyprus	▪
Japan	▪
Japan	▪
Greece	▪
NetherInd	▪
Japan	▪
Bulgaria	▪
Bulgaria	▪
Japan	▪
Lithuania	▪
Russian F	▪
Japan	▪
Czech R	▪

Population 2 (cont.)

Country	Page Area of Textbook
Slovak R	▪
Germany	▪
Argentina	▪
Dom Rep	▪
NetherInd	▪
South Af	▪
China	▪
Japan	▪
South Af	▪
Japan	▪
South Af	▪
Portugal	▪
Hungary	▪
Hungary	▪
Lithuania	▪
Russian F	▪
Japan	▪
Scotland	▪
N Zealnd	▪
Slovenia	▪
SwitzerInd	▪
Iran	▪
Lithuania	▪
Russian F	▪
SwitzerInd	▪
N Zealnd	▪
Romania	▪
Portugal	▪
Australia	▪
Romania	▪
SwitzerInd	▪
Philippins	▪
Greece	▪
SwitzerInd	▪
Sweden	▪
Argentina	▪
NetherInd	▪
Spain	▪

Science Textbooks (cont.)

Population 3

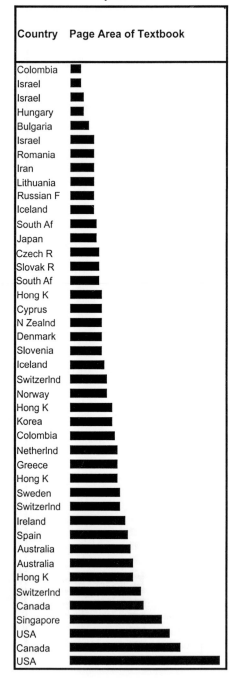

Country	Page Area of Textbook
Colombia	
Israel	
Israel	
Hungary	
Bulgaria	
Israel	
Romania	
Iran	
Lithuania	
Russian F	
Iceland	
South Af	
Japan	
Czech R	
Slovak R	
South Af	
Hong K	
Cyprus	
N Zealnd	
Denmark	
Slovenia	
Iceland	
Switzerlnd	
Norway	
Hong K	
Korea	
Colombia	
Netherlnd	
Greece	
Hong K	
Sweden	
Switzerlnd	
Ireland	
Spain	
Australia	
Australia	
Hong K	
Switzerlnd	
Canada	
Singapore	
USA	
Canada	
USA	

Population 2 (cont.)

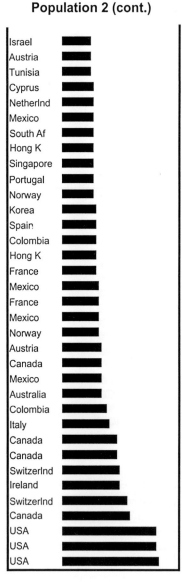

Israel
Austria
Tunisia
Cyprus
Netherlnd
Mexico
South Af
Hong K
Singapore
Portugal
Norway
Korea
Spain
Colombia
Hong K
France
Mexico
France
Mexico
Norway
Austria
Canada
Mexico
Australia
Colombia
Italy
Canada
Canada
Switzerlnd
Ireland
Switzerlnd
Canada
USA
USA
USA

Exhibit 2.9 provides a sense of the varying dimensions of textbooks, with photographs of actual textbooks from the United States, Norway, and China (pictured from the top down).

Exhibit 2.9   Variation in the Physical Sizes of Textbooks

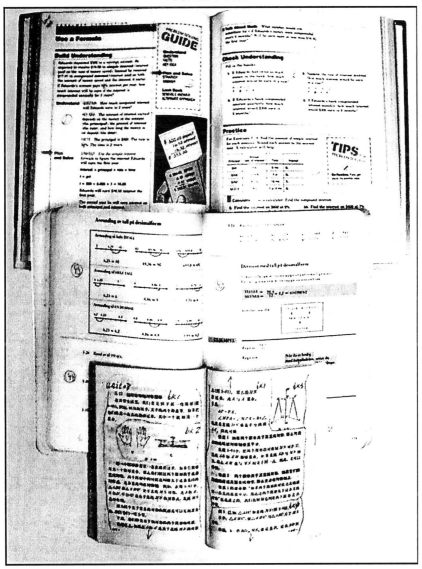

Graphics

The use of visual aids such as photographs, pictures, tables, and graphs varies substantially from textbook to textbook and provides still another indicator of how textbooks vary in their physical features. Such variation reflects on the degree to which textbooks rely on the visual presentation of the mathematics or science content in addition to the written word. Its presence could enhance the presentation of certain mathematics or science content such as geometry or forces and motion. Exhibit 2.10 provides a table of the distribution of the varying amounts of graphical content (expressed as percents) as well as boxplots of these distributions.[12]

From this display it is apparent that there is a substantially larger proportion of graphical material in science textbooks compared to mathematics books. This was true regardless of the age group for which the textbook was intended. In fact, there is little variation in the amount of graphics across the three populations. The median for mathematics indicated around 10 percent of the textbook was made up of graphics. Science textbooks had three times that amount.

A question that arises when examining these data is whether or not the 'information density' of graphic material is different across intended student populations or subject matters. One indication of greater density would be if more content or performance expectation codes were associated with the graphic material. Examination of Exhibit 2.11 however, suggests that, in general, this is not the case. The number of content codes required to characterize graphics material increases slightly in textbooks intended for progressively older student populations but the number of necessary performance expectation codes decreases. However, the variation from population to population is small and the difference between mathematics and science textbooks does not appear to be noteworthy.

Exhibit 2.10   Distribution of Percent of Graphics Blocks in Textbooks

	Population	Number of Textbooks	mean	Standard Deviation	Minimum	Median	Maximum	Distribution
Mathematics Textbooks	1	72	13%	9%	0%	11%	35%	
	2	72	12%	11%	0%	9%	46%	
	3	50	12%	7%	0%	13%	31%	
Science Textbooks	1	60	35%	14%	8%	34%	79%	
	2	120	34%	12%	12%	33%	71%	
	3	44	35%	11%	13%	34%	61%	

Exhibit 2.11   Average Number of Codes Per Graphics Blocks for Lesson Units

Number of Content Codes for Each Graphic Block

	Population	Number of Textbooks	Average	Standard Deviation
Mathematics Textbooks	1	71	1.06	0.31
	2	71	1.19	0.35
	3	50	1.31	0.70
Science Textbooks	1	60	1.27	0.31
	2	120	1.31	0.37
	3	44	1.42	0.41

Number of Performance Expectation Codes for Each Graphic Block

	Population	Number of Textbooks	Average	Standard Deviation
Mathematics Textbooks	1	71	1.12	0.42
	2	71	1.13	0.39
	3	50	1.09	0.53
Science Textbooks	1	60	1.05	0.17
	2	120	1.08	0.19
	3	44	1.03	0.09

However, we can consider not only the *number* of performance expectations embedded in graphics material but also how *complex* those performance expectations are. The situation is different when we consider the relative complexity of the performances that graphics are intended to elicit from students. For example, we might ask whether the use of graphics intended that students simply inspect and understand the information

Exhibit 2.12   Performance Expectations Associated with Graphic Materials in Textbooks

Mathematics Textbooks

Graphic Characteristics of Textbooks	Population 1 (71 Textbooks)				Population 2 (71 Textbooks)				Population 3 (50 Textbooks)			
	Mean	Std Dev	Minimum	Maximum	Mean	Std Dev	Minimum	Maximum	Mean	Std Dev	Minimum	Maximum
Percentage of graphic blocks with more complex performance expectations	9.7	15.4	0.0	58.3	9.9	17.9	0.0	75.0	7.2	16.5	0.0	71.0
Percentage of other blocks with more complex performance expectations	21.6	17.5	0.0	83.4	36.6	26.0	0.0	98.2	45.5	26.2	5.6	97.0
Percentage of all blocks with more complex performance expectations	20.0	15.6	0.0	69.1	33.0	23.3	0.0	82.4	40.5	23.7	3.8	94.6

Science Textbooks

Graphic Characteristics of Textbooks	Population 1 (60 Textbooks)				Population 2 (120 Textbooks)				Population 3 (44 Textbooks)			
	Mean	Std Dev	Minimum	Maximum	Mean	Std Dev	Minimum	Maximum	Mean	Std Dev	Minimum	Maximum
Percentage of graphic blocks with more complex performance expectations	3.1	6.0	0.0	27.1	4.9	9.0	0.0	55.0	8.8	21.9	0.0	94.8
Percentage of other blocks with more complex performance expectations	13.8	14.7	0.0	61.0	15.4	15.2	0.0	63.6	28.5	17.4	0.0	73.1
Percentage of all blocks with more complex performance expectations	10.1	10.8	0.0	42.5	11.7	11.2	0.0	40.9	21.5	14.8	0.0	68.2

contained in them or whether the graphics form part of the textbook writer's effort to have students engage in formulating and clarifying problems and situations. Exhibit 2.12 shows some of the differences between mathematics and science textbooks.

The overall percentage of textbook blocks designed to elicit more complex performances from students increased in mathematics textbooks intended for use by students at higher grade levels. The mean percent for Population 3 was double that for Population 1. However, examination of only those blocks with graphics showed very little change in the complexity of performance expectations across the populations. In fact the figure for Population 3 was slightly lower than that for both Populations 1 and 2.

Science was different. The percentage of all block types with more complex performance expectations increased for textbooks at the higher grade levels, as was the case for mathematics. In science, however, this pattern was also true for graphics blocks. Apparently graphics serve a different pedagogical purpose in science textbooks than in mathematics textbooks. For the most part, graphics material in textbooks generally tends to provide primarily information and not to demand more complex student behaviors but this is more true in science at least in Populations 1 and 2. Also, science textbooks only demand such complex behaviors half again as much as do mathematics textbooks when considering the whole book not just the graphical material.

This chapter has focused on the most salient physical features of TIMSS textbooks – part of their macro structure. The variation in these physical features, especially the more extreme cases, raises the hypothesis that such characteristics could impact the degree to which the intended vision – the content – would be realized as teachers and students engage with the textbook. If true, this would likely alter the corresponding opportunities to learn and, given statistical modeling reported elsewhere, the amount learned. How discrete content and activity elements in textbooks as described in this chapter are incorporated into sequences and structures is the story developed in the next chapter. The characterization of the variation in textbook size across the "TIMSS world" portends a complexity and diversity in textbooks that will be explored more fully throughout this book.

Notes:

[1] TIMSS Population 1 consisted of the two adjacent grades containing the majority of nine-year-olds. TIMSS Population 2 consisted of the two adjacent grades containing the majority of thirteen-year-olds. The textbook analysis focused on the upper grade for each pair of grades.

[2] A complete listing of all textbooks included in the TIMSS study can be found in Schmidt et al. 1997b (Appendix G) and Schmidt et al. 1997c (Appendix G). Of the original 630 books that are listed in these references, 130 of them came from only two countries (Switzerland and Scotland). We felt that this imbalance would result in a few countries dominating the statistical summaries such as the mean and, hence, the characterization of what was typical in the "TIMSS world." We therefore reduced the set of textbooks that were actually analyzed by randomly selecting only a sample of those from Switzerland and Scotland as an attempt to reduce the potential bias. Additionally, around 80 of the books were eliminated from analyses because they were supplemental documents, teachers guides, workbooks, or textbooks not part of the original design (e.g., secondary biology books). This reduced the set to the 418 reported in this book. The number of textbooks varies slightly for some analyses reflecting idiosyncrasies of particular textbooks that renders them inappropriate for certain analyses. In structure, these anomalies likely represent randomly missing data.

[3] This textbook was used in Israel at the time of TIMSS but has now been replaced by a new book.

[4] Schmidt et al. 1996; Schmidt et al. 1997b, Schmidt et al. 2001.

[5] Schmidt et al. 1997a; Valverde and Schmidt 2000; Schmidt et al. 2001.

[6] Schmidt et al. 2001.

[7] Survey of Mathematics and Science Opportunities 1992a; Survey of Mathematics and Science Opportunities 1992b; Survey of Mathematics and Science Opportunities 1992c; Survey of Mathematics and Science Opportunities 1992d.

[8] What follows is adapted from a summary of the procedures originally outlined in Appendices B and E of Schmidt et al 1997b, pages 200-204.

[9] Survey of Mathematics and Science Opportunities 1992b; Survey of Mathematics and Science Opportunities 1992c; Robitaille et al. 1993.

[10] These aspects are further explained in Appendix A and in subsequent chapters.

[11] Although block 5 appears to be a graphics block, this is a chemical equation and equations are considered to be part of the narrative both in science and mathematics.

[12] A boxplot, sometimes referred to as a 'box and wiskers' plot, is a graphical representation of a distribution of numbers. The "box" encloses the middle 50 percent of values, ranging from the 25th percentile to 75th percentile. The line in the box indicates the median or 50th percentile value. The lines at either end of the box, the 'wiskers', mark the middle 90 percent of values ranging from the value associated with the fifth percentile to that associated with the 95th percentile.

Chapter 3
Textbook Structure

Mathematics and science textbooks are written to influence how teachers and students use their instructional time throughout the school year. Content standards and similar policy instruments lay out a set of instructional goals. Across countries they do so with greater or lesser specificity. Textbooks are designed to translate such goals into practice at a much more specific level. Even when the goals and their specificity are the same across countries or within the same country, the precise manner in which these goals are sequenced in textbooks will likely vary. This is the "signature" of a textbook, its own particular interpretation of the best structure by which to present the prescribed content. As a consequence, textbooks propose a sequence of pedagogical situations and content. By doing so they attempt to exert influence on the decisions that teachers make in developing the content specified in the content standards. We argue that this could influence how effectively students will learn that content.

Teachers reported in the TIMSS questionnaires that textbooks were a primary information source in deciding how to present content.[1] Textbooks even had a major impact on decisions about what to teach and also on practical decisions about which instructional approach to follow and which exercises to use in class. Textbooks were the dominant source of information for planning what to teach in five of the 26 countries and the second most often cited by teachers in eight other countries. Other factors also influenced these decisions. However textbooks were one of the few pedagogical tools the teacher shared with students. As a result it affected what could be and was accomplished in the classroom.

There are a variety of structures in which the content and activities of a textbook can unfold. Teachers in their own instruction can use an even greater variety of such structures. However, we believe that there is a strong likelihood that the actual classroom instructional sequence is related to the sequence proposed in the textbooks. That is, we believe that actual classroom experiences are influenced by what we have termed the structure of the textbook. The data show that textbooks differ in the patterns of presentation of their various elements. They also differ in the way in which various elements are integrated with each other.

Textbook form and structure advance a distinct pedagogical model. That is, they embody a plan for the particular succession of educational opportunities considered optimal for enacting curricular intentions. An understanding of the form and structure of textbooks permits uncovering the model of instruction that textbooks embody and provides a first examination of how textbooks promote distinctive configurations of educational opportunities in the classroom.

The TIMSS curriculum analysis included ways to examine the form and structure – what might be called the "morphology" – of textbooks as wholes. In this chapter we address the question of identifying such textbook morphologies. We attempt to characterize textbooks in terms of how they incorporate content, performance expectations, and presentation formats into pedagogical structures.

To depict these structures we developed a type of graphical analysis that can represent the general manner in which the elements of textbooks were sequenced. That is, these graphical displays provide an illustration that portrayed the sequence of content for an entire textbook. We term these visual displays "schematics." These schematics were analyzed to develop a classification scheme describing different types of structures that appeared across approximately 400 textbooks analyzed in TIMSS.

SCHEMATIC REPRESENTATION OF TEXTBOOKS

Exhibit 3.1 presents a schematic for a mathematics textbook intended for the use of Population 1 students. The schematic lays out the summary of the textbook's structure on a vertical series of three grids. The upper grid corresponds to block types. These are the "rhetorical" characterizations of the textbook's blocks (i.e.: narrative, graphic, etc.) which characterize the presentation format. The rows represent the possible block types; the columns represent the blocks themselves. A vertical hash mark is placed for each occurrence of the block type in question. Bold lines are provided to mark separations between textbook lessons. In this case the textbook contains 14 lessons. If done as designed, each lesson should correspond to from one to approximately three days of instruction, in which case this particular book is intended for less than a year's worth of instruction or else each lesson is designed to last for more than three days.

Separated by a space, a second grid corresponding to the content is in the middle position. Here the row represents the various topics and, again, the columns indicate separate blocks. Each hash line marks the presence of a particular topic in a particular block.[2] Blocks can, and often do, have more than one content code assigned to them so there is often more than one hash line in the same column.

Finally, the grid in the bottom position uses hash marks to indicate which performance expectation is present in each block. Again there is often more than one of these used to characterize the same block and thus more than one hash mark sharing the same column. Successive columns characterize successive blocks throughout the book. Each of the three grids parallels the others. Scanning vertically provides information on each block and scanning horizontally provides information on how the textbook unfolds from the first page to the last.

Exhibit 3.1   A Schematic Representation of Textbooks

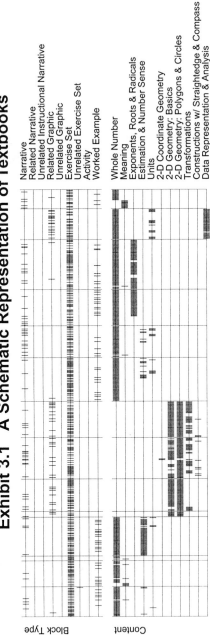

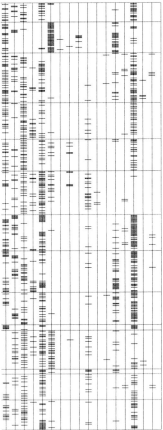

In this example we have a mathematics textbook in which the majority of the mathematics is conveyed through exercises, with much less material included in the form of narrative, graphics and worked examples. There is also a clear set of content emphases – most of the textbook addresses whole number topics, with extensive coverage as well of basic two-dimensional geometry and polygons and circles.

In these lessons students are mostly expected to demonstrate knowledge by representing mathematical situations, recalling mathematical properties, performing routine procedures, or using mathematical vocabulary and notation. However, the schematic also discloses that within this textbook there are five lessons that differ from the others. Three of these lessons are the only ones in which there is a substantial amount of material conveyed through graphics; these lessons all deal with geometry. These same lessons also have a preponderance of the expectation that students use mathematical vocabulary and notation.

The second-to-last lesson in this textbook is also distinct. It deals with data representation and analysis (combined with whole number topics). It contains more material than is typical for this book in which students are expected to use more complex mathematical procedures and to engage in conjecturing as a form of mathematical reasoning. This is likely associated with investigating patterns in the representations of data.

To understand the differences that these schematics unveil, we turn our attention to a Spanish mathematics textbook intended for the same age group. Its schematic is presented in Exhibit 3.2. This textbook contains many more lessons then the previous one – a total of 52. In this textbook there is no primary emphasis for conveying the mathematical content. Mathematics is conveyed mostly through narrative, graphics, exercises and worked examples. The textbook begins with lessons on mathematical set theory and then moves to the topic of operations with whole numbers. Some material addressing other number concepts (associated with different number bases) interrupts this; the text then resumes the emphasis on operations with whole numbers. Following this is text on common fractions followed by decimal fractions. This material is succeeded by text dealing with the concept of measurement units, interrupted by some material on basic two-dimensional geometry, after which measurement topics resume. The final lessons deal with polygons and circles.

Another distinctive feature of this textbook is that most of the lessons contain a set of blocks that deal with recurring mathematical content. One is the topic of whole number operations – which receives sustained treatment in a number of lessons as well. The other is the topic of estimating computations – a topic that recurs throughout the textbook, but which is not the primary focus of any one lesson.

Exhibit 3.2   Schematic of a Spanish Population 1 Mathematics Textbook

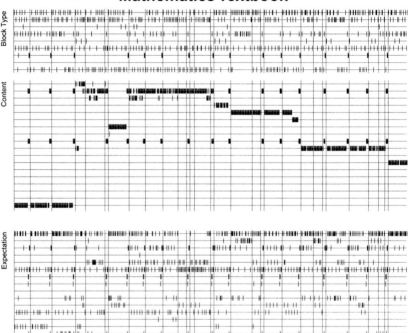

In contrast to these two very different mathematics textbooks, consider the following depiction of a science textbook from Korea (Exhibit 3.3) intended for the same age group. Here, science is conveyed only through graphics and activities. If implemented as designed, the pedagogy of that science class would be very different from that of the pedagogy implied by the Spanish mathematics textbook.

The textbook begins with lessons dealing with the topic of light followed by those dealing with bodies of water (a topic in earth science). Succeeding these lessons on bodies of water are the only lessons in the book that integrate more than one topic from the TIMSS frameworks simultaneously. These lessons cover the topics of the classification of matter, as well as its physical and chemical properties. The lessons go about the integration of these topics by accretion. First comes material dealing solely with the classification of matter and then material integrating such

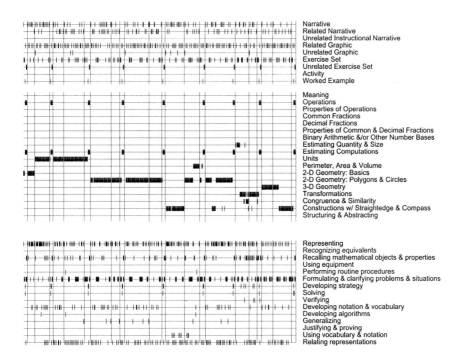

Exhibit 3.3   Schematic of a Korean Population 1 Science Textbook

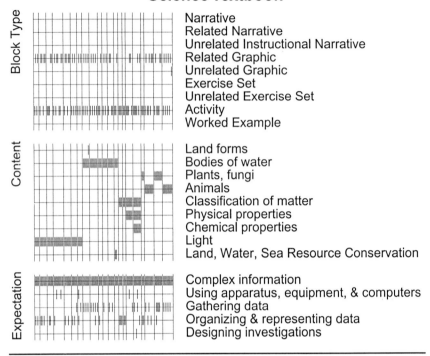

classification with physical properties. Finally, there is material integrating all three topics. Following the physics topics are lessons that address plants, fungi, and animals.

Across the book, students are expected to understand complex information (information that integrates simple information); gather data; and organize and represent data. These latter two expectations are consistent with the rhetorical style of the book and together suggest a very "hands on" or empirical pedagogical approach.

Such a textbook is quite different from the Russian Federation science book intended for Population 2 students, shown in Exhibit 3.4. This textbook deals first and foremost with one topic – zoology. Some material regarding evolution and speciation, animal morphology (organs, tissues), and life cycles accompany the primary emphasis on animals and types

Exhibit 3.4   Schematic of a Russian Population 2 Science Textbook

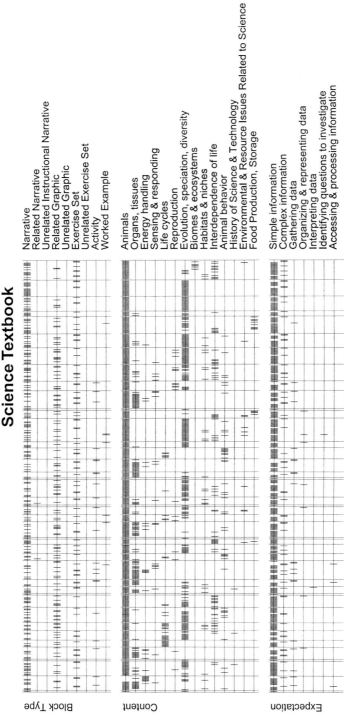

of animals. Most of the material is conveyed through narrative and graphics. There are many question sets – and students are primarily expected to read and understand simple information such as vocabulary, facts and simple concepts. A much smaller proportion of the textbook expects that students will understand complex information or gather data.

PATTERNS IN THE SEQUENCING OF CONTENT

Content is one basis for the classification of textbook structure using the schematics. Most of the textbooks can be characterized by one of three approaches to content sequencing (although, as in most classification schemes, individual textbooks exhibit some level of deviance from the overall pattern defining the category to which it belongs).

The first type of textbook is one in which there is essentially only one content theme for the entire book. The term "content theme" is not synonymous with "topic" since a theme can be made up of several topics that are logically intertwined. Themes can be identified by the presence of the sustained treatment of a single topic by itself or in combination with other topics. In terms of the schematic used to portray the textbooks, the single content theme would be visible by the presence of one or a small number of relatively continuous black lines across the whole textbook. These black lines could exhibit breaks (discontinuities) and still be considered a theme if the breaks are few and their duration (in terms of the number of pages) is small.

For textbooks with single content themes but multiple topics, the schematic could have a small number of black lines representing logically connected topics from a disciplinary point of view which are essentially parallel to each other. Alternatively it could have a small number of black lines representing logically connected topics which alternate with each other over the book. As in all data analysis minor deviations from the pattern are considered as merely perturbations from the general pattern.

The other two types of textbooks have more than one dominant theme. The first of these has a clear and orderly succession of identifiable but different content themes across the book. The schematics in this case have sustained black lines as in the first category of textbooks but these lines do not cover the whole book. By contrast there are several points where the black line stops after covering a sizable portion of the book and a new line begins to represent the next theme in a sequenced fashion.

The third category of textbooks has a number of topics each scattered across the textbook without a clear pattern of succession. It is impossible to discern particular themes from these textbooks. They are, at best, collections of topics, which confer them with an encyclopedic quality. The schematic in this case would have many short black lines with little or no apparent pattern.

Category 1: Textbooks with one Dominant Content Theme

Textbooks that address a single content theme are relatively uncommon in the "TIMSS world", representing approximately 10 percent of all textbooks.[3] Textbooks that address essentially only one content theme and one that can be characterized with only one dominant code from the TIMSS content framework are exceptionally uncommon. They constitute less than half of the textbooks that address only one content theme.

Single Topic Themes. Examples of these types of textbooks are presented in Exhibit 3.5. Here we see two mathematics textbooks. One is from the Russian Federation and intended for Population 1 and focuses almost entirely on operations with whole numbers with only an occasional inclusion of another topic such as units of measurement. The other is a mathematics textbook from Israel intended for Population 2 students. That textbook is devoted essentially to the coverage of patterns, relations and functions with only a smattering of other topics (such as slope).

Multiple-Topic Themes. More common among the one-themed textbooks were those in which the themes were complex enough to require more than one TIMSS content code to fully characterize them. This is different from the pattern found in the textbooks illustrated in Exhibit 3.5 in which the additional topic not defining the theme does not have sustained coverage and is not mathematically necessary to define the theme. For example, in the Russian textbook, measurement units is not covered in a very continuous way as it has many breaks in its coverage and is not logically necessary to define the theme; as such it does not warrant being included in the definition of the theme. Multiple-topic theme textbooks were somewhat more common among advanced mathematics textbooks intended for a college-preparatory course in the final year of secondary school than was true for other student populations and subjects. Two examples, one from Hong Kong the other from Mexico are presented in Exhibit 3.6.

The textbook from Hong Kong is mostly a calculus textbook that focuses throughout the year on the content topics of infinite processes

Exhibit 3.5 Examples of Content Schematics For Textbooks With a Single Dominant Content Theme (Single Topic)

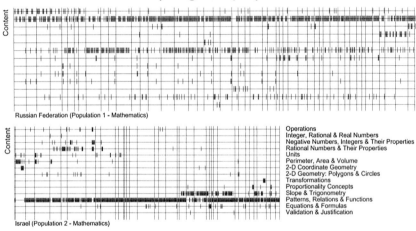

Russian Federation (Population 1 - Mathematics)

Israel (Population 2 - Mathematics)

Operations
Integer, Rational & Real Numbers
Negative Numbers, Integers & Their Properties
Rational Numbers & Their Properties
Units
Perimeter, Area & Volume
2-D Coordinate Geometry
2-D Geometry: Polygons & Circles
Transformations
Proportionality Concepts
Slope & Trigonometry
Patterns, Relations & Functions
Equations & Formulas
Validation & Justification

and change although there is occasional coverage of geometry and algebra topics throughout the book which likely serve as context and applications for the calculus. This is an example of where the topics making up the content theme mostly alternate with each other.

The Mexican textbook also has one content theme but that theme is far more complex. The book builds a three-part theme by beginning with equations and formulas, and then incorporating both the calculus topic of change and the algebra topic of relations and functions in the early lessons. After pursuing this three-faceted theme for more than half the book, a final thematic component – perimeter, area and volume – is incorporated with the other topics, likely reflecting the incorporation of conic sections. This is an example where the topics defining the theme are intertwined and run in parallel to each other.

Meaning
Operations
Properties of Operations
Common Fractions
Rounding & Significant Figures
Units
Perimeter, Area & Volume
2-D Geometry: Basics
2-D Geometry: Polygons & Circles
Constructions w/ Straightedge & Compass
Proportionality Problems
Equations & Formulas
Data Representation & Analysis

Exhibit 3.6   Examples of Content Schematics
For Textbooks With One Dominant Content Theme
(Multiple Topics)

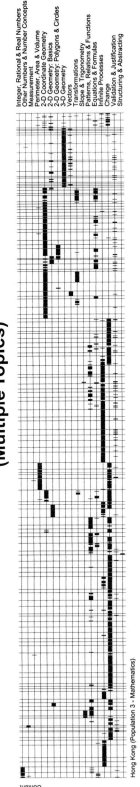

Hong Kong (Population 3 - Mathematics)

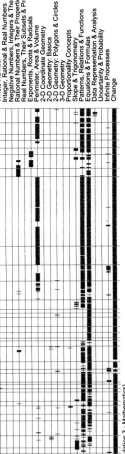

Mexico (Population 3 - Mathematics)

Category 2: Textbooks Reflecting a Progression of Sequential Themes

Most TIMSS textbooks – approximately 60 per cent – are structured to provide an orderly progression of successive content themes intended for coverage across the book. We distinguish between three types of sequential-theme textbooks: multiple topic, single topic, and recursive single topic.

Multiple Topic Themes. Only about five percent of the textbooks with sequential themes have ones that are characterized by more than one TIMSS content code. Exhibit 3.7 shows two such examples both of which are science textbooks. One is from Denmark and intended for Population 1. The other is from France and intended for Population 2. In the case of the textbook example from Denmark, a consistent succession of multiple topic themes is evident going first from lessons devoted to the structure and organization of plants and animals, to those covering life processes and the interdependence of life. These themes are then succeeded by animals in ecosystems, and moves finally to the life cycles of plants. After these themes with multiple topics the rest of the book progresses with a succession of single-topic themes.

The French physical science textbook also shows a succession of multiple-topic themes. However, the first half of the book addresses two single-content themes in succession, first electricity and then light. Following these, the lessons take up multiple-topic themes incorporating the classification and physical properties of matter, gradually incorporating physical changes and their explanations, and then following with a theme made up of the physical and chemical properties of matter combined at different points with the topic of atomic structure.

Recursive single-topic themes. More common than successive,

Exhibit 3.7   Examples of Content Schematics For Textbooks With Sequential Themes (Multiple Topics)

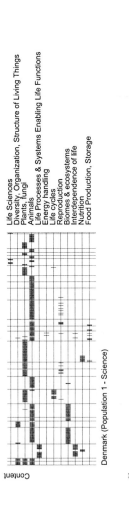

Denmark (Population 1 - Science)

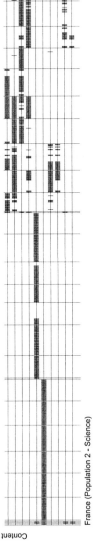

France (Population 2 - Science)

Exhibit 3.8   An Example of a Content Schematic For Textbooks With Sequential Themes (Interspersed with a Recurring Topic)

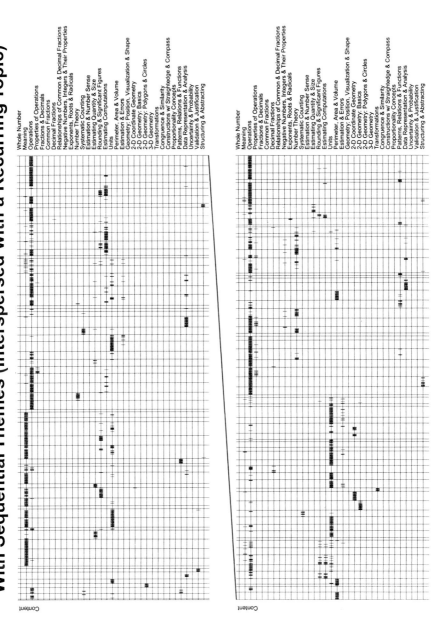

Exhibit 3.8 cont.

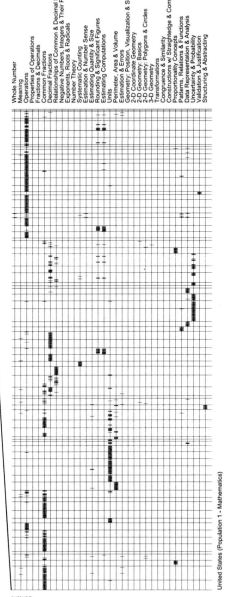

United States (Population 1 - Mathematics)

multiple-topic theme textbooks are those which have successive single-topic themes but ones in which some themes reappear at intervals throughout the book. These recursive themes were present in about 30 percent of the textbooks that exhibited successive themes. Exhibit 3.8 presents an example from the United States. The size of the schematic reflects the large number of pages in US textbooks (see Chapter 2).

In the US Population 1 textbook, lessons return regularly after covering other topics to the topic of operations with whole numbers. This occurs throughout the whole book. The first lesson focuses on operations and after moving to the topic of whole number meaning again returns to operations. This pattern repeats itself over ten times (counting only the shifts to other topics that encompass a fairly large segment of the book – counting all shifts, the number is much larger) with the only difference being that the intermediate topic is different each time. The implied pedagogical model behind this textbook is one of intermittent reinforcement of the topic that serves as the dominant theme of the book.

Single-topic themes. Most books that are built up of successive content themes do not revisit themes at intervals throughout the book. These books have lessons that move from one focus to another in a clearly identifiable sequence. Good examples of this type of textbook are those from Sweden and the Russian Federation seen in Exhibit 3.9.

In the Swedish textbook intended for college-bound mathematics students in their final year of secondary school, there are about eight major themes sequenced throughout the book. Near the beginning of the book there is a lesson with no discernable single theme but, other than this lesson, the basic structure of the textbook is to progress through these eight themes one at a time, completing each before moving on to the next one. This is in marked contrast to the US mathematics book described in the previous section and this structure clearly has a different type of implied pedagogy than that of the US Population 1 textbook.

Exhibit 3.9   Examples of Content Schematics For Textbooks With Sequential Themes (Single Topics)

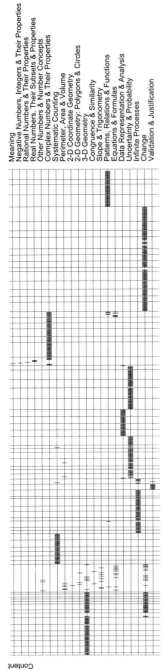

Sweden (Population 3 - Mathematics)

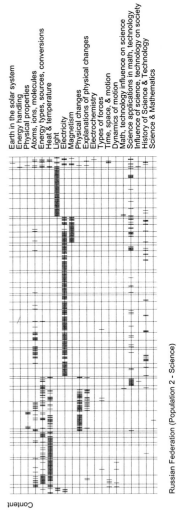

Russian Federation (Population 2 - Science)

The Russian Federation Population 2 science textbook has only four successive themes. The book begins with the topic of heat and temperature (combined at times with energy types), moves to physical changes (coupled with heat and temperature), and then concludes with electricity followed by light. At one point several of the lessons consider magnetism together with electricity.

Category 3: Textbooks with Fragmented Content Coverage

Around 30 percent of the almost four hundred TIMSS textbooks exhibited a fragmented pattern of content coverage. That is, they moved among numerous topics in what appeared to be a disjointed manner. These textbooks appeared to only rarely – if at all – take up a content theme for a succession of lessons. The general pattern is one of brief coverage of a topic interrupted by similar short coverage of other topics only to return to a series of such brief encounters with the original topics. In the schematic, this appears as a series of short segments (almost like points) instead of the longer segments (lines) that characterized the category 2 textbooks.

For some textbooks, a small number of clusters of lessons sharing content themes were isolated among lessons with no apparent interrelationships. Such an approach seemed common in the Norwegian science textbooks. A different type of fragmentation is apparent in other textbooks. This is relatively common among textbooks in the United States, for example, which mostly provided isolated coverage across a large number of disconnected topics. As a part of this there was often much repetition of the same topic but not treated continuously in one section of the book but rather spread across the book in a disjointed fashion. Examples of textbooks exhibiting this pattern are presented in Exhibit 3.10.

Exhibit 3.10 Examples of Content Schematics For Textbooks With Fragmented Content Coverage

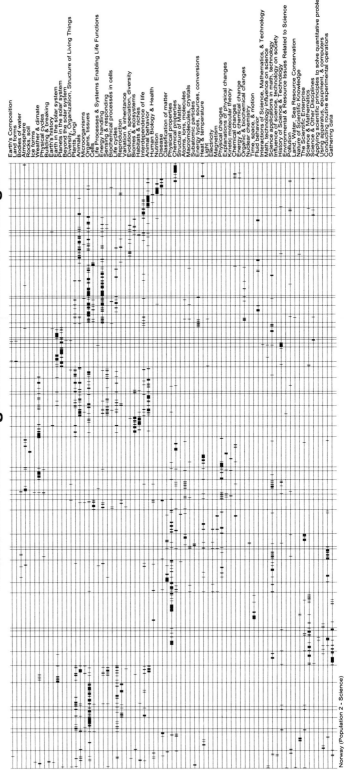

Norway (Population 2 - Science)

Exhibit 3.10   cont.

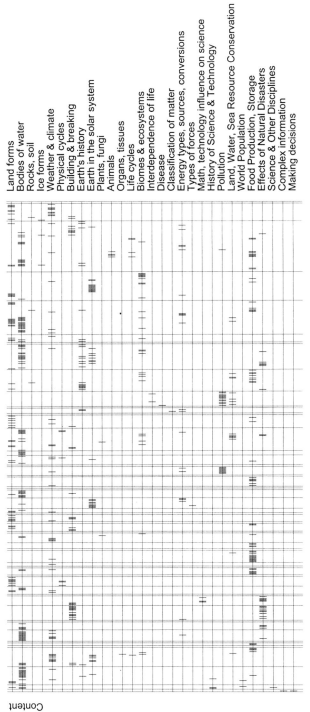

Switzerland (Population 2 - Science)

COUNTRY MEMBERSHIP AND THE CONTENT TYPOLOGY

An examination of Exhibit 3.11 reveals that the majority of several countries' textbooks are of one type in the content typology. This is true no matter the grade for which the textbook is intended. Japan is a good example. Around 70 percent of its textbooks are best represented by category 2 – a succession of content themes – and there are no Japanese textbooks of the fragmented type.

Several countries have almost all (around 90 percent or more) of their textbooks belonging to a single category. This is true for Australia, Colombia, the Dominican Republic, Singapore, South Africa, Spain, Tunisia, and Scotland. All of these mostly have textbooks that are structured by a succession of content themes. On the other hand, for the United States, Canada, Iceland, Mexico, Norway, Portugal, Sweden, and Thailand half or more of their books have a fragmented content structure.

Only around twenty-five percent of the countries have textbooks belonging to all three categories. For seven of the countries the distribution of their textbooks across the three categories is statistically significantly different from the overall distribution ($p < .05$). The countries for which this is true include Canada, Israel, the US, Japan, Mexico, Switzerland, and South Africa.

PATTERNS IN THE SEQUENCING OF PERFORMANCE EXPECTATIONS

An examination of performance expectations in TIMSS textbooks reveals two distinct approaches. Most textbooks either concentrate predominately on the same performance expectations across lessons or, alternatively, progress successively across lessons from one set of performance expectations to another.

Exhibit 3.11   Country Distribution of Textbooks in Each Content Typology

Country	Number of Textbooks	Percent of Textbooks with One Dominant Theme	Percent of Textbooks with A Progression of Sequential Themes	Percent of Textbooks with Fragmented Themes
Argentina	4	0	75	25
Australia	12	0	92	8
Austria	6	0	67	33
Bulgaria	9	22	56	22
Canada	20	0	45	55
China	10	10	50	40
Colombia	12	0	92	8
Cyprus	7	0	71	29
Czech Republic	10	10	70	20
Slovak Republic	8	0	75	25
Denmark	6	33	33	33
Dominican Republic	3	0	100	0
France	5	0	80	20
Germany	6	17	83	0
Greece	10	10	70	20
Hong Kong SAR	15	13	67	20
Hungary	9	0	67	33
Iceland	8	13	25	63
Iran	8	0	75	25
Ireland	7	0	86	14
Israel	16	38	31	31
Italy	8	0	100	0
Japan	16	31	69	0
Korea	6	0	83	17
Mexico	9	0	33	67
Netherlands	15	13	40	47
New Zealand	7	0	57	43
Norway	6	0	50	50
Philippines	4	0	75	25
Portugal	6	0	33	67
Romania	8	13	50	38
Russian Federation	10	20	50	30
Singapore	7	0	100	0
South Africa	15	7	93	0
Spain	10	0	90	10
Sweden	6	0	50	50
Switzerland	20	35	45	20
Thailand	2	0	50	50
Tunisia	2	0	100	0
Scotland	2	0	100	0
USA	19	0	42	58
Slovenia	7	0	71	29
Total	376	9	63	28

Textbooks with Homogenous Performance Expectations across Lessons

Most TIMSS textbooks exhibit consistency in their emphasis on a single set of performance expectations. Approximately 65 percent of the books are of this type. Most of the lessons in those books attempt to elicit the same types of performances from students as those that precede them and those that follow. In some cases, the performance expectation emphasis is primarily on one TIMSS performance expectation. Exhibit 3.12 illustrates textbooks of this type.

In each case there is a concentration on one of the TIMSS performance expectation codes. These emphases – the high priority performance expectation for that year of study and subject – are different in each case. They range from the emphasis on understanding simple facts, definitions and vocabulary in the case of the US science textbook, to integrating, comparing and contrasting information (complex information) in the case of the Japanese text intended for the same student population.

Exhibit 3.12   Examples of Schematics For Textbooks With Homogenous Performance Expectations (Single Code)

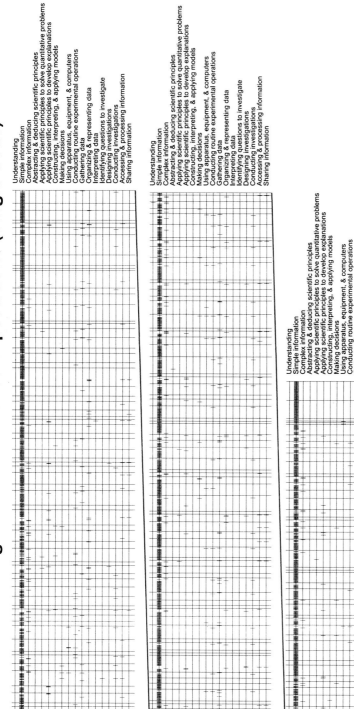

United States (Population 2 - Science)

Exhibit 3.12   cont.

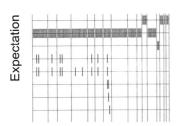

Expectation

Simple information
Complex information
Thematic information
Using apparatus, equipment, & computers
Conducting routine experimental operations
Gathering data
Organizing & representing data
Interpreting data

Japan (Population 2 - Science)

Other textbooks emphasize more than one performance expectation consistently across lessons. Exhibit 3.13 illustrates this with examples from the Russian Federation and Hong Kong. In the example from the Russian Federation (for Population 2 students) lessons consistently emphasize the representation of mathematical objects and procedures as well as justification and proving. In the textbook from Hong Kong (intended for the final year of college-preparatory mathematics), the lessons concentrate on recall and performing routine procedures.

Textbooks with Performance Expectation Emphases Changing in Progression across Lessons

Although less common, a number of textbooks have changing performance expectations that progress in succession across lessons much like the successive content themes noted earlier. In these books, a performance expectation or set of expectations is emphasized for a number of lessons, and then a new group of lessons concentrates on a different set of expectations. In some cases, this change of performance expectations is recursive, with the textbook's lessons returning to performance expectations at intervals across the lessons.

Exhibit 3.13   Examples of Schematics For Textbooks With Homogenous Performance Expectations (Multiple Codes)

Russian Federation (Population 2 - Mathematics)

Representing
Recalling mathematical objects & properties
Using equipment
Using more complex procedures
Solving
Developing notation & vocabulary
Generalizing
Justifying & proving
Using vocabulary & notation
Describing/discussing

Knowing
Representing
Recognizing equivalents
Recalling mathematical objects & properties
Using equipment
Performing routine procedures
Using more complex procedures
Formulating & clarifying problems & situations
Solving
Developing algorithms
Generalizing
Conjecturing
Justifying & proving
Using vocabulary & notation
Relating representations
Describing/discussing
Critiquing

Hong Kong (Population 3 - Mathematics)

Knowing
Representing
Recognizing equivalents
Recalling mathematical objects & properties
Using equipment
Performing routine procedures
Using more complex procedures
Formulating & clarifying problems & situations
Solving
Developing algorithms
Generalizing
Conjecturing
Justifying & proving
Using vocabulary & notation
Relating representations
Describing/discussing
Critiquing

Expectation
Expectation
Expectation

Exhibit 3.14   Examples of Schematics For Textbooks With Recursive Performance Expectations

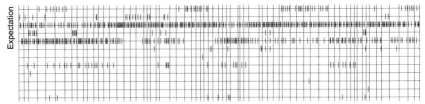

Scotland (Population 1 - Mathematics)

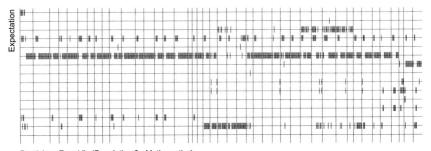

Dominican Republic (Population 2 - Mathematics)

This is the case of the books illustrated in Exhibit 3.14. The mathematics textbook from Scotland (for Population 1 students) emphasizes recall throughout all lessons, but a concentration on performing routine procedures and solving problems recurs at intervals across lessons. In the case of the mathematics textbook from the Dominican Republic (intended for Population 2 students), lessons alternate between a concentration on the performance of routine procedures and demonstrating the correct use of specialized mathematical terminology and notation.

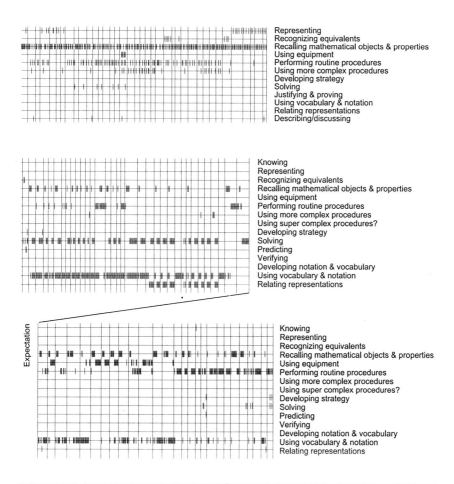

A number of textbooks present lessons without this recursiveness. That is, the performance expectation foci change in succession without subsequently returning to the same performance expectations later in the text. An example of this type of succession is presented in Exhibit 3.15. The advanced mathematics textbook from the Netherlands for the end of secondary school emphasizes two types of performance expectations in succession. First it concentrates on the performance of routine procedures. This is followed by lessons in which students are expected to recall mathematical objects and properties fitting given conditions.

Exhibit 3.15   An Example of a Schematic For Textbooks With Successive Performance Expectations

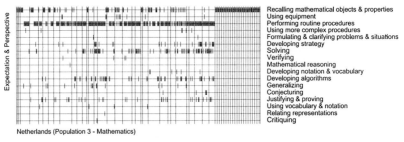

Netherlands (Population 3 - Mathematics)

Expectation & Perspective

Recalling mathematical objects & properties
Using equipment
Performing routine procedures
Using more complex procedures
Formulating & clarifying problems & situations
Developing strategy
Solving
Verifying
Mathematical reasoning
Developing notation & vocabulary
Developing algorithms
Generalizing
Conjecturing
Justifying & proving
Using vocabulary & notation
Relating representations
Critiquing

Multiple Performance Expectations in a Single Lesson

Most textbooks contain performance expectation emphases that reveal patterns such as those described in the preceding sections. However, a few textbooks address a wide array of performance expectations across their lessons. Exhibit 3.16 represents one such type. Some textbooks – such as the science textbook from Singapore – appear to contain lessons that consistently attempt to elicit a complex variety of performance expectations from students. A large number of focused expectations consistently occur throughout the textbook. In this case, the lessons regularly include in addition to understanding simple information, a number of expectations relating to students using apparatus, routine procedures, and science processes, investigating the natural world, and communicating.

PATTERNS IN SEQUENCING THE PRESENTATION FORMATS

Each lesson in a textbook was subdivided into blocks as described in Chapter 2. Recall that these blocks were characterized according to how they presented the material. Presentation formats were characterized as being narrative (central, related, unrelated, and sidebar instructional narrative); graphic (graphic blocks related to narrative or informative graphic blocks not directly related to instructional narrative); exercise and question sets (either directly related to a unit's content or unrelated – for

Exhibit 3.16   An Example of a Schematic With Multiple Lesson Performance Expectations

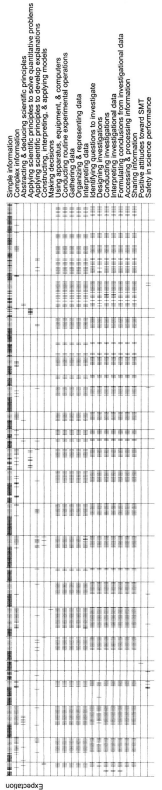

Singapore (Population 2 - Science)

Exhibit 3.17   An Example of a Textbook Schematic With a Single Presentation Format

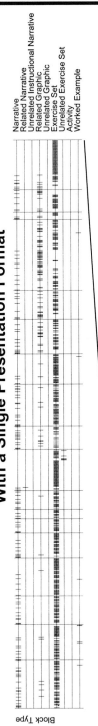

Italy (Population 2 - Mathematics)

example review sets inserted as part of a lesson on a different topic); suggested activities; worked examples of algorithms and formulas; and "other" textbook block types.

The data reveal important patterns in block types across TIMSS textbooks. One common pattern – largely characteristic of mathematics textbooks – is the concentration on the presentation of the content in a single predominant way. Thus, the Italian textbook portrayed in Exhibit 3.17 shows a common pattern in mathematics textbooks of emphasis on the use of exercise sets in teaching school mathematics. There are other textbooks with a similarly singular approach to conveying subject matter. One example is a science textbook from the US in which the majority of the material takes the form of graphics.

More commonly, textbooks concentrate on a small set of rhetorical methods for conveying content and eliciting student performances. Exhibit 3.18 presents examples from three countries. The examples from both Sweden and Austria are textbooks intended for school science for Population 2 students. In the Swedish textbook, content is presented almost exclusively as narrative or in related graphics. In the case of the Austrian textbook, lessons concentrate on four methods for presenting science content – narrative, related graphics; exercises and question sets; and activities. In the Chinese mathematics textbook for Population 2 content is conveyed mostly through graphics and exercises.

Recursive presentation formats – that is, textbook material that concentrates on different presentation formats in different sections of the textbook, also occur but somewhat less frequently. Exhibit 3.19 shows an example. Here is a mathematics textbook from the Russian Federation (intended for Population 2 students) in which lessons present mathematics through narrative and 'side bar' or parallel narrative alternating with exercises.

Exhibit 3.18   Examples of Schematics For Textbooks With Multiple Presentation Formats

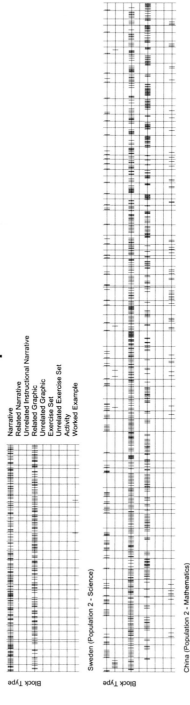

Exhibit 3.19   An Example of a Textbook Schematic With Recursive Presentation Formats

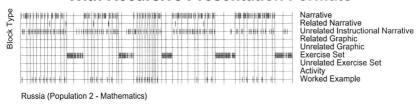

Block Type

Narrative
Related Narrative
Unrelated Instructional Narrative
Related Graphic
Unrelated Graphic
Exercise Set
Unrelated Exercise Set
Activity
Worked Example

Russia (Population 2 - Mathematics)

AN INTEGRATED LOOK ACROSS CONTENT, PERFORMANCE EXPECTATIONS AND METHODS OF PRESENTATION

The preceding discussion has explored how the different parts of these schematics reveal groups of textbooks sharing analogous approaches to either the exploration of content, the eliciting of student performances, or the use of distinct rhetorical tools for conveying school mathematics or science. In the case of most textbooks in the TIMSS sample, these components of the schematic run in an unrelated fashion to each other. Visual inspection does not note apparent relationships between patterns of, for example, presentation of content and eliciting student performances. They do not appear to reveal preferences in the textbooks for presentation of particular content focusing on specific performance expectations deemed of highest priority for that content or for that block type.

In Exhibits 3.1 – 3.4 at the beginning of this chapter, visual inspection clearly does not reveal patterns in which, for example, a certain content is presented in a certain type of block. There is no clear pattern of whether certain block types (for example, exercises) are more likely to attempt to elicit one set of performance expectations than other block types.

However, there are a small number of exceptions. In a textbook from Israel, when lessons concentrate on the use of exercises or question sets, they also concentrate much more on having students provide evidence for the validity of an action or the truth of a statement. This is sought by an appeal to mathematical results or properties, or by an appeal to logic – which is what is meant by the performance expectation of "justifying and proving". This does not appear to depend on the content topic addressed in the textual material.

A different relationship between content, performance expectations and block types appear in a textbook from Singapore. At intervals in this textbook, lessons appear to take on a fragmented approach to content – losing the thematic focus of other portions of the book. When this occurs, the lessons concentrate on exercises and question sets that in turn concentrate on students performing routine procedures.

However, these types of patterns are infrequent. Most books in TIMSS appear to have only occasional instances of patterns of content presentation, performance expectation or presentation formats that appear to vary with the particular content or performance expectations. Most appear to advocate a 'generic' approach to school mathematics and science – one in which textbook morphology remains largely invariant across contents or performance expectations. Thus these data reveal considerable variation in contents, block types, performance expectations, and in their sequences and combinations. There do not appear to be characteristic structural combinations relating these factors.

Notes:

[1] Schmidt et al. 2001.

[2] Refer to the definition of block provided in chapter 2.

[3] For all analyses reported in this section, the subject matter of the textbook or the age/grade level was regarded as unimportant, since the manner in which pedagogical situations are presented across the course of study is the focus. Thus, mathematics and science textbooks intended for all three focal populations are included together in the classification scheme.

Chapter 4

Content Presentation

In the previous chapter we examined the general ways in which textbooks organize and sequence content, expectations for student performance, and presentation formats or "implied" instructional activities. We posited three types of content structures into which the textbooks were classified. This aspect of form and style seems particularly relevant to our hypothesis that such characteristics could be more or less effective in facilitating the learning of the content contained in the book. This is especially the case since form here involves the sequencing of the content itself. In this chapter we examine other features of the form and style associated with textbook content. We argue that these too are features that are critical to a realization of the opportunities a textbook is designed to provide because of their closeness to the content itself.

We first examine measures of the amount of content contained in textbooks. We then examine the extent to which different textbooks are aligned with the "TIMSS world" core contents in mathematics and science –contents that exist across a large proportion of textbooks in the "TIMSS world."

A third aspect of structure closely related to the discussion of sequence in Chapter 3 examines the degree of "choppiness" or fragmentation associated with the presentation of the content. To explore this we introduced the analytical device of a textbook *strand*. This is defined as a sequence of textbook material that has the same mathematics or science content as its focus. Thus a strand defines a thematic whole and is distinguishable from other strands by a change in content.[1] The focus in this chapter is on the number of times the theme changes – or, more simply, on the number of strands. This in effect describes the fluidity or continuity of the document since textbooks with many strands or "breaks" in their flow would be much less fluid to read. That is, there would be many discontinuities in the book. This characteristic is visible in the schematics presented in the previous chapter.

In the final part of this chapter we turn to another aspect of the way in which content is structured in textbooks. We examine how abstractly content is conveyed, not in terms of the abstractness of the content itself but in terms of its presentation – concrete examples and representations versus a more formal and abstract system of text and symbols.

AMOUNT OF CONTENT

We begin with a look at one of the simpler components of textbook content structure – the number of mathematics or science topics in a textbook. This is an indicator that describes the number of disciplinary 'points' the textbook is intended to make and thus helps characterize its structure at least in terms of the amount of implied learning activity embedded in the text.

Mathematics

Exhibit 4.1 portrays the distribution of the number of topics included in the mathematics textbooks for each of the student populations.[2] These graphs are important because they demonstrate how textbooks intended for students of the same age, studying the same school subject, differ vastly in the number of content elements incorporated in their structure. In the case of textbooks for Population 1, most textbooks contain from 12 to 20 topics. The average number is 17 but a few textbooks contain more than 30 topics.

In Population 2 the average number of topics is 24 but unlike Population 1 there is much greater variability across textbooks. Most textbooks contain from 12 to 30 topics. Textbooks from a few countries, most notably the US and Canada, contain many more topics (over 30) than

Exhibit 4.1   Number of Topics in Mathematics Textbooks by Population

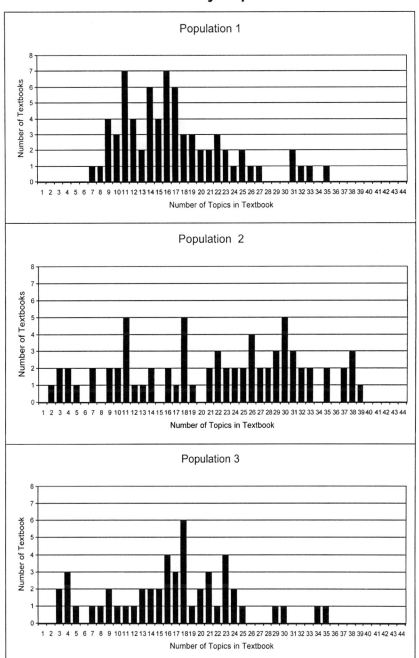

is common across the sample. This was true for both Populations 1 and 2. An examination of these distributions reveals how truly uncommon such textbooks are. There are some textbooks with fewer than ten topics intended for each of the three populations. (However, it should be noted that there are a few textbooks in the sample not meant for a full year of instruction).

For secondary school students studying advanced mathematics in their final year, the textbooks are typically less comprehensive in topic coverage than those for Population 2. This may well be largely because these textbooks focus on specific contents deemed as prerequisites for work in mathematics at the post-secondary level. In these textbooks the average number of topics is approximately 18.

Exhibit 4.2, deals with these same characteristics but only for Population 2 mathematics textbooks (eighth grade in the United States and for most countries). In this case the textbooks are organized according to the national sample to which they belong. Additionally, textbooks are adjusted to represent the course of study for a full year. Thus we may validly compare textbooks in countries such as Japan, which uses two textbooks over the course of a year, with other countries for which yearlong instruction uses only one textbook.

Here we observe that Latvia, Switzerland, and the US (followed closely by Canada) on average had textbooks covering the largest number of topics. Switzerland is a special case. When the books were averaged to represent Switzerland as a whole, the aggregation was taken over textbooks from the three distinct language systems involved in Swiss education. As such the number of topics overestimates what a typical student in any one of the educational systems was likely to experience in his or her textbooks.

Bulgaria, Germany, and Japan clearly had textbooks intending coverage of fewer topics than typical for most TIMSS countries. In fact, their textbooks on average covered less than half the number of topics

Exhibit 4.2   Number of Mathematics Topics Included in Population 2 Textbooks

Country	Number of Topics (44 possible topics)
Australia	30
Austria	26
Bulgaria	14
Canada	39
Colombia	34
Cyprus	17
Czech Republic	32
Slovak Republic	32
Denmark	21
France	31
Germany	15
Greece	30
Hong Kong	23
Hungary	30
Iceland	27
Iran	22
Ireland	33
Israel	24
Japan	15
Korea	18
Latvia	44
Netherlands	28
New Zealand	27
Norway	31
Portugal	35
Romania	32
Russian Federation	19
Singapore	21
South Africa	28
Spain	27
Sweden	28
Switzerland	42
Scotland	28
USA	41
Slovenia	25

covered in the countries with the most comprehensive textbooks such as the United States.

Certainly these tables point to mathematics textbooks that are different in terms of the magnitude of the learning tasks they imply. However, the number of topics included in textbooks is possibly a misleading indicator of the magnitude of these tasks. It is likely that although textbooks contain many topics, some receive sustained treatment while others are mentioned only in a cursory manner. Sustained treatment would indicate a different set of instructional possibilities from cursory or tangential mentioning. We next gauge this difference.

Exhibit 4.3 indicates the number of topics needed to cover at least 80 per cent of each textbook in the sample. This is one way to obtain an indication of "sustained treatment." A small number indicates that a major portion of the textbook is devoted to covering a limited number of topics and thus likely represents sustained treatment of each. A large number indicates a textbook that has a more encyclopedic approach. That is, such a book attempts to cover a larger number of topics and must, on average, cover each more cursorily. These indicators are again summarized as distributions.

Important differences in textbooks are seen in how sustained and focused topics are treated. For Population 1, around 60 percent of the books devoted sustained treatment to no more than 5 topics. This number changes to six topics in Population 2 and four topics in the case of the mathematics specialist students of Population 3. For end of secondary school almost 70 percent of the textbooks have four or fewer topics encompassing 80 percent of the book. The countries that are anomalies here are the same as in the previous section. For example, the US books have among the largest number of topics necessary to cover 80 percent of the book – eight at fourth grade, 13 at eighth grade (up to 17 for one book), and four at the end of secondary school.

Exhibit 4.3   Percentage of Mathematics Textbooks That a Specific Number of Topics to Cover 80% of the Textbook

Number of Topics Needed	Population 1 Percentage	Population 2 Percentage	Population 3 Percentage
1		9.7	12.0
2	14.3	8.3	22.0
3	7.1	13.9	16.0
4	21.4	8.3	20.0
5	17.1	8.3	24.0
6	12.9	11.1	2.0
7	10.0	8.3	
8	8.6	2.8	4.0
9	2.9	5.6	
10	4.3	4.2	
11	1.4	2.8	
12		6.9	
13			
14		4.2	
15		2.8	
16		1.4	
17		1.4	
18			
	100.0	100.0	100.0

Science

Exhibit 4.4 depicts the distribution of the number of topics in science textbooks and parallels Exhibit 4.1. It is common for these textbooks to cover slightly more topics than is the case for mathematics in Population 1. The average number of topics for Populations 1 and 2 is approximately 25 while the average is around three for the Population 3 physics textbooks. Thus the Population 3 science specialists textbooks have many fewer topics than the corresponding mathematics textbooks (which had an average of 18 topics).

Exhibit 4.4   Number of Topics Included in Science Textbooks by Population

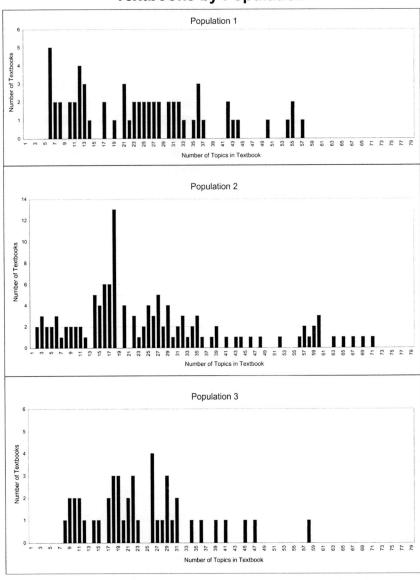

Exhibit 4.5, shows these same characteristics for eighth grade science textbooks, organized by the national sample to which they belong and adjusted to represent a year's course of study. Fewer topics are intended in Denmark, Iran, and Japan than in most other TIMSS countries. This is also true for Japan's eighth grade mathematics textbooks and may be a

cultural phenomenon. Canada, Switzerland and the United States commonly have textbooks that cover substantially more topics than other TIMSS countries during a year's course of school science. This was also true for mathematics textbooks in Canada and the US.

Exhibit 4.5   Number of Science Topics Included in the Textbooks

Country	Number of Topics (79 possible topics)
Australia	65
Austria	60
Bulgaria	57
Canada	74
Colombia	65
Cyprus	53
Czech Republic	49
Slovak Republic	49
Denmark	9
France	37
Germany	32
Greece	49
Hong Kong	37
Hungary	62
Iceland	46
Iran	19
Ireland	58
Israel	32
Japan	17
Korea	38
Latvia	35
Netherlands	67
New Zealand	52
Norway	61
Portugal	64
Romania	53
Russian Federation	42
Singapore	27
South Africa	49
Spain	67
Sweden	49
Switzerland	78
Scotland	44
USA	78
Slovenia	62

Looking at the sustained treatment of topics in Exhibit 4.6 for science (paralleling Exhibit 4.3 for mathematics), school science textbooks clearly are slightly more comprehensive than mathematics textbooks. For fourth grade about 65 percent of the textbooks have seven or fewer topics make up 80 percent of the book. The comparable numbers for eighth grade and end of secondary school are six in both cases.

There is a tendency for US textbooks (both in mathematics and science) to have a more comprehensive approach to the number of topics included in textbooks for students in the younger TIMSS populations. In contrast, at the end of secondary school while many countries have textbooks with a large number of topics, US textbooks have relatively fewer topics. In mathematics this may be explained by the fact that the US college-bound population focuses work almost exclusively on calculus. The reason in science is less clear.

COMMON CONTENT THEMES

A question that has received considerable attention in TIMSS is identifying those mathematics and science topics that receive the most cross-national attention for each of the populations studied. This resulted in the determination of a 'world core' of contents intended by 70 per cent of the TIMSS countries at each population.[3]

These 'world core' topics essentially represent a set of 'world' themes in school mathematics and science (at least according to the "world of TIMSS"). Determining how much of each textbook's content is devoted to this 'core' helps gauge the characteristic nature of a book from a content point of view – how much its priorities share the content priorities of the textbooks from a substantial number of other countries. The extent to which this differs appreciably from the core for a given textbook indicates to what extent it is idiosyncratic in its topic coverage and, hence, indicates a book that provides opportunities that are different from that to which most

Exhibit 4.6   Percentage of Science Textbooks that Require a Specific Number of Topics to Cover 80% of the Textbook

Number of Topics Needed	Population 1	Population 2	Population 3
	Percentage	Percentage	Percentage
1	1.7	8.3	2.3
2	6.7	7.5	9.1
3	16.7	13.3	4.5
4	11.7	12.5	11.4
5	10.0	10.0	22.7
6	10.0	15.0	22.7
7	6.7	7.5	9.1
8	8.3	5.8	13.6
9	10.0	5.8	2.3
10	5.0	4.2	
11	5.0	2.5	2.3
12	1.7	0.8	
13	1.7	0.8	
14	1.7		
15	3.3	0.8	
16		0.8	
17		1.7	
18			
19			
20		1.7	
21		0.8	
	100.0	100.0	100.0

students in the "TIMSS world" are being exposed. Another way to say this is that this measure identifies unique books at least from a content point of view.

Mathematics

Exhibits 4.7 through 4.9 present box plots which represent the distributions of the percentage of space each textbook in the sample devotes to each of the mathematics topics most commonly presented in textbooks across the "TIMSS world" at each of the three populations.

Exhibit 4.7 World Core Topic Coverage in Population 1 Mathematics Textbooks

World Core Topics*	Number of Textbooks with No Coverage	Average Coverage	Standard Deviation	Minimum	Maximum	Distribution
Whole Number Meaning	11	10%	10%	0%	38%	
Whole Number Operations	1	13%	10%	0%	40%	
Properties of Whole Number Operations	14	9%	15%	0%	78%	
Common Fractions	11	10%	10%	0%	38%	
Measurement Units	1	13%	10%	0%	40%	
Measurement : Perimeter, Area & Volume	17	5%	5%	0%	15%	
2-D Geometry: Basics	18	5%	6%	0%	26%	
2-D Geometry: Polygons & Circles	14	5%	6%	0%	27%	

* Seventy Population 1 Mathematics Textbooks were used in this analysis.

Exhibit 4.8 World Core Topics Coverage in Population 2 Mathematics Textbooks

World Core Topics*	Number of Textbooks with No Coverage	Average Coverage	Standard Deviation	Minimum	Maximum	Distribution
Negative Numbers, Integers & Their Properties	24	4%	5%	0%	24%	
Rational Numbers & Their Properties	27	5%	13%	0%	100%	
Exponents, Roots & Radicals	26	4%	6%	0%	28%	
Measurement : Perimeter, Area & Volume	19	6%	7%	0%	35%	
2-D Coordinate Geometry	17	4%	5%	0%	22%	
2-D Geometry: Basics	15	6%	8%	0%	37%	
2-D Geometry: Polygons & Circles	11	11%	13%	0%	63%	
3-D Geometry	29	6%	14%	0%	93%	
Geometry: Transformations	28	4%	7%	0%	41%	
Proportionality Problems	21	4%	12%	0%	100%	
Patterns, Relations & Functions	20	8%	13%	0%	90%	
Equations & Formulas	13	19%	21%	0%	83%	
Data Representation & Analysis	21	4%	5%	0%	21%	

* Seventy-two Population 2 Mathematics Textbooks were used in this analysis.

Exhibit 4.9   World Core Topics Coverage in Population 3 Mathematics Textbooks

World Core Topics*	Number of Textbooks with No Coverage	Average Coverage	Standard Deviation	Minimum	Maximum	Distribution
2-D Coordinate Geometry	9	7%	8%	0%	30%	
Patterns, Relations & Functions	2	28%	27%	0%	99%	
Equations & Formulas	0	25%	19%	2%	82%	
Elementary Analysis: Infinite Processes	2	12%	8%	0%	33%	
Elementary Analysis: Change	4	31%	22%	0%	74%	
Validation & Justification	15	8%	14%	0%	76%	
Other Math Content	15	4%	8%	0%	46%	

* Forty-three Population 3 Mathematics Textbooks were used in this analysis.

These data indicate that there are distinct country patterns for incorporating the commonly intended content in mathematics. Textbooks for fourth graders allocated vastly different amounts of space to the world core topics, especially the topic of whole number operations. Some country's entire books essentially focused on specific 'world core' topics. Examples include an Austrian textbook, a textbook of the Czech Republic, and all of the Canadian textbooks which all focused on operations with whole numbers. In one case this content constituted almost 80 percent of the book.

Another Austrian textbook focused primarily on whole number operations from among the world core topics, but also focused substantially on the topics of common fractions, measurement units, and the measurement topic of 'perimeter area and volume'. Some coverage of whole number operations was common across the textbook sample but the amount varied and in a one case the textbook did not cover the topic at all (i.e., one of the textbooks from Singapore).

Other countries have mathematics textbooks that pursue a more integrated treatment across multiple world core topics. Textbooks from Israel focus on all three commonly intended topics in whole numbers. This is also true for textbooks from the Dominican Republic and two textbooks from Hong Kong. They share the focus on whole number topics characteristic of Israeli texts, but also incorporate a focus on common fractions. All four Hong Kong textbooks share a substantial focus on common fractions.

At eighth grade the two world core topics with the greatest variability include one from algebra (equations and formulas) and one from geometry (polygons and circles). Some books are predominantly about equations with this content constituting up to 80 percent of the book. Others are essentially about polygons and circles (over 60 percent of the book). It should be kept in mind that these two topics are only part of algebra and geometry respectively.

Several countries intend mathematics instruction to be conveyed in two textbooks for thirteen-year-old students. The two books focus separately on algebra and geometry. – This is true for the People's Republic of China, the Czech Republic, Israel, and the Russian Federation. Other countries have single textbooks with a dual focus on these areas (for example, Spain). In Korea and Japan textbooks concentrate on algebra but give little emphasis to the geometry topics commonly included in other TIMSS countries. Japan does have a focus on geometry but the topic is congruence and similarly, which is not part of the world core. In the US there is no substantial focus on any of the commonly intended topics. In fact, focus, whether on commonly intended or other contents, is not a characteristic of US textbooks overall.

For Population 3 the amount of coverage for the world core topics varies tremendously over the world's textbooks. They are mostly about analysis, equations, and functions yet the amount of coverage varies from no coverage to essentially the entire book.

Elementary mathematical analysis was one of the commonly included topics for students receiving the most demanding curriculum in mathematics in the final year of secondary school. The books vary in the degree to which this topic was included in them. For example, elementary analysis is the focus of textbooks in Colombia and Cyprus, in one of the Iranian textbooks, and in Japan. Israel has three types of textbooks in its national sample – one that focuses extensively on elementary analysis (the topic of change), one that focuses on algebra (two books), and one that combines a substantial focus on both algebra and elementary analysis as well as the topic of validation and proof.

Science

Exhibits 4.10 through 4.12 provide the same type of data for science textbooks. TIMSS countries commonly covered elements of botany and zoology for nine-year-olds. In both cases the variation was large ranging from no coverage to around half of the book. Many countries have textbooks

Exhibit 4.10   World Core Topics Coverage in Population 1 Science Textbooks

World Core Topics*	Number of Textbooks with No Coverage	Average Coverage	Standard Deviation	Minimum	Maximum	Distribution
Weather & climate	27	3%	5%	0%	28%	
Earth in the solar system	27	4%	5%	0%	19%	
Plants, fungi	12	13%	12%	0%	48%	
Animals	11	13%	14%	0%	59%	
Organs, tissues	17	10%	14%	0%	75%	
Interdependence of life	24	3%	5%	0%	32%	
Physical properties	27	5%	8%	0%	43%	
Energy types, sources, conversions	33	3%	9%	0%	65%	
Land, Water, Sea Resource Conservation	27	3%	4%	0%	26%	

* Sixty-one Population 1 Science Textbooks were used in this analysis.

Exhibit 4.11 World Core Topics Coverage in Population 2 Science Textbooks

World Core Topics*	Number of Textbooks with no Coverage	Average Coverage	Standard Deviation	Minimum	Maximum	Distribution
Rocks, Soil	80	3%	6%	0%	26%	
Weather and Climate	73	6%	17%	0%	88%	
Plants, Fungi	75	3%	7%	0%	41%	
Animals	63	5%	15%	0%	100%	
Organs, Tissues	63	7%	12%	0%	66%	
Sensing and Responding	70	2%	4%	0%	26%	
Life Cycles	76	2%	7%	0%	49%	
Independence of Life	77	2%	6%	0%	50%	
Disease	68	2%	6%	0%	38%	
Classification of Matter	58	4%	7%	0%	35%	

Physical properties	50	4%	7%	0%	56%	
Chemical properties	62	6%	15%	0%	100%	
Atoms, Ions, Molecules	57	3%	5%	0%	24%	
Energy Types, Sources, conversions	50	4%	6%	0%	35%	
Heat and Temperature	67	3%	5%	0%	23%	
Light	70	3%	8%	0%	37%	
Electricity	72	8%	19%	0%	100%	
Types of Forces	77	2%	4%	0%	22%	
Applications of Science in Mathematics and Technology	53	3%	6%	0%	33%	
Influence of Science, Technology on Society	73	1%	2%	0%	16%	
Pollution	58	1%	2%	0%	10%	
Conservation of Land, Water, and Sea Resources	55	1%	2%	0%	15%	
Conservation of Material and Energy Resources	72	1%	2%	0%	15%	

* One hundred and twenty Population 2 Science Textbooks were used in this analysis.

Exhibit 4.12　World Core Topics Coverage in Population 3 Science Textbooks

World Core Topics*	Number of Textbooks with No Coverage	Average Coverage	Standard Deviation	Minimum	Maximum	Distribution
Subatomic particles	5	6%	9%	0%	46%	
Energy types, sources, conversions	1	10%	7%	0%	28%	
Wave phenomena	4	11%	11%	0%	60%	
Sound & vibration	11	4%	5%	0%	27%	
Light	4	11%	11%	0%	53%	
Electricity	5	24%	19%	0%	85%	
Magnetism	7	10%	9%	0%	33%	
Quantum theory & fundamental particles	11	7%	9%	0%	50%	
Types of forces	9	7%	9%	0%	37%	
Time, space, & motion	8	10%	11%	0%	44%	
Dynamics of motion	9	8%	9%	0%	33%	

* Forty-four Population 3 Science Textbooks were used in this analysis.

that emphasize both areas. This includes the Czech and Slovak Republics, Denmark, Ireland, and South Africa. Other countries (such as Japan and Singapore) emphasized botany more. Focusing more on zoology was less common. Only one textbook from Canada, one from Switzerland, those from the Netherlands and those from Norway do this. Textbooks in the Dominican Republic, Hungary and one from Hong Kong complement a focus on botany and zoology with treatment of the life science topic of organs and tissues.

Organs and tissues is the most commonly intended topic in one textbook covering three-fourths of the book. It is also the most commonly covered topic for books from Hong Kong, Israel, and Switzerland. Israel and Japan are the only countries with textbooks substantially focusing on the physical sciences for this age group. One Israeli book devotes more than half of its space to the topic of energy types, sources and conversions. Both of Japan's textbooks have substantial treatment of the physical properties of matter.

At eighth grade (Population 2) the TIMSS textbooks were similarly highly variable in their coverage of the world core topics. Organs and tissues, weather and climate, electricity, chemical properties and animals were among the most variable. For the topics electricity, animals, chemical properties and weather and climate, the range of coverage went from no coverage to virtually (and in three cases literally) the entire book covering the topic.

The coverage devoted to the most demanding physics curriculum in the last year of secondary school also varied. The topic with the greatest variation in coverage was electricity, which was also the most variable topic for eighth graders. In Denmark and Hungary students have books that emphasize quantum theory. This is complemented in Denmark with treatment of the topic types of forces. In Hungary it is complemented with more treatment of atomic structure. Textbooks from Israel are distinct in their large emphasis on wave phenomena.

Another way to examine the data summarized in Exhibits 4.7 to 4.12 is to characterize each textbook as to the percent of the book that covers the world core topics in total. If this percentage is small, then the textbook can be considered as idiosyncratic in its content coverage at least with respect to the "TIMSS world." In effect, such a small percentage implies that the textbook mostly covers topics not common to 70 percent of the TIMSS countries.

In mathematics, there are no such Population 1 textbooks as all of them have 50 percent or more devoted to covering the core topics. At Population 2, there are a handful of such textbooks. These include books from Tunisia, Sweden, and Switzerland. Even at Population 3, there are several such textbooks, the most notable of which are three textbooks from Iran, Mexico, and Russia for which the percent covering core topics is less than 10 percent.

The reason for such low coverage of the core topics can be two fold. In one case, the number of topics can be large covering most of the possible topics and, as a result, much of the book covers non-core topics. The other possibility is that the book focuses on a smaller number of topics but ones that differ from the core topics.

This is illustrated by two eighth grade mathematics textbooks, one from Japan and one from the United States. The Japanese book covers few topics but 40 percent of the book covers non-core topics. A US textbook has the same non-core coverage (40%) but covers many more topics.

Science is different in that there are many more such unique textbooks in terms of their content coverage when compared to other TIMSS countries. This is true at Populations 1 and 2 but not Population 3 in which there are fewer such textbooks in comparison with mathematics. Even in Population 1, there are some 20 textbooks with coverage of core topics at less than 50 percent of the book. For Population 2, the most unique science textbooks come from Switzerland, Hong Kong, Japan, Argentina, Romania, and China where only about one-fourth of the book covers the core topics.

The differences between mathematics and science textbooks in this regard likely reflects the fact that science is multiple-discipline based and therefore permits greater topic variation. It also perhaps reflects less international agreement in terms of what constitutes school science.

CONTENT STRANDS: A MEASURE OF FOCUS

Content strands are portions of textbooks in which the content over instructional units or blocks is the same. Thus, strands denote the succession of instructional elements in textbooks that share a common content focus or theme.

Examining the number of content strands in textbooks allows us to identify one feature of the structure of textbooks – how often content themes change. This characterizes how often there is a break in the content "flow" of the textbook. This is not the same as the earlier measures of the number of topics in a book. If each topic were covered once in a single strand in the textbook then the number of topics and number of strands would be the same. If the number of strands is larger than the number of topics then some topics occur in more than one strand. In this way books with very large numbers of strands (since the number of potential topics is limited) represent a high frequency of leaving and returning to a topic.

In some textbooks, these content strands are few, quite long, and encompass many blocks. In others, the strands are short and numerous. The first case indicates building content themes in a focused manner. Essentially each new central theme builds on foundations laid by the content preceding it. The second indicates an irregular approach in which it is more common for content themes to keep changing and repeating over the book.

The sustained and irregular approaches no doubt present very different pedagogical challenges to teachers. It is certainly reasonable to hypothesize that this aspect of structure is closely related to the degree to which the content presented in this way is likely to be learned.

Mathematics

Exhibit 4.13 presents data on the number of content strands for mathematics textbooks in the sample (country names are used for each textbook from that country that was analyzed) for all three populations. The mean number of content strands or "breaks" – that is, the number of times within each textbook that a content strand ends and a new one begins – varies little across populations. The mean number is 46 in textbooks intended for fourth graders, and is 54 and 55, respectively, for textbooks intended for eighth graders and for advanced mathematics students in their final year of secondary school. This suggests a relatively invariant approach to structuring content themes in textbooks that is not dependent on the specific contents in them. This is part of what we called the macro structure of textbooks.

However, there is a tremendous variation among books within each population. In textbooks for both Populations 1 and 2, the US had textbooks with by far the largest number of content strands or breaks. The number of such breaks in some US textbooks is around ten times the potential number of content themes if the book were organized to cover each topic a single time. Canada's textbooks are the most similar to the US's in this regard for Population 1.

As stated above, on average the number of times that the mathematics 'story' changes emphasis for fourth graders is 46 times. The US and Canadian textbooks include from one and a half to six times as many changes in focus. Textbooks from Korea, the Netherlands, the Philippines, and Israel have many fewer breaks in their textbooks than the cross-textbook

Exhibit 4.13   Number of Strands or Breaks in Mathematics Textbooks

Population 1

Country	No. of Breaks
USA	307
USA	202
Canada	175
USA	142
Australia	127
USA	122
Mexico	120
Canada	113
Latvia	104
Spain	94
Canada	93
Bulgaria	87
Ireland	82
Australia	77
Canada	72
Hungary	65
Slovenia	61
Switzerland	58
South Africa	54
Norway	45
Dominican Republic	42
South Africa	41
Thailand	41
Colombia	40
Iran	40
Norway	40
Colombia	35
France	34
Russian Federation	34
Scotland	32
Spain	32
Ireland	30
Romania	29
Iceland	27
Japan	27
New Zealand	27
Italy	26
Japan	26
Japan	25
Portugal	24
Italy	23
Greece	22
Hong Kong	22
Japan	22
Hong Kong	21
Korea	21
Korea	20
Czech Republic	18
Israel	18
Slovak Republic	18
Singapore	18
Austria	15
China	14
China	13
Hong Kong	13
Cyprus	12
Israel	12
Iceland	11
Switzerland	11
Switzerland	11
Austria	10
Singapore	10
Cyprus	9
Hong Kong	9
Denmark	8
Israel	6
Korea	5
Korea	5
Netherlands	5
Philippines	4

Population 2

Country	No. of Breaks
USA	215
USA	195
Sweden	186
Colombia	178
USA	151
USA	139
Iceland	133
USA	129
Canada	128
Norway	125
France	114
Canada	106
Switzerland	97
Greece	83
Ireland	76
New Zealand	76
China	75
Bulgaria	74
Thailand	73
Austria	72
Switzerland	68
Tunisia	64
Korea	63
Bulgaria	53
Hong Kong	53
Australia	51
Dominican Republic	50
Mexico	47
Germany	44
South Africa	42
Switzerland	41
Hungary	40
Netherlands	40
Sweden	39
Austria	38
Philippines	38
Israel	37
Colombia	36
Switzerland	35
Slovenia	34
Spain	34
Denmark	33
Italy	33
Russian Federation	31
South Africa	31
Cyprus	30
Iran	27
Israel	27
Czech Republic	24
Japan	24
Slovak Republic	24
Singapore	22
Spain	21
Netherlands	20
Romania	20
Netherlands	19
Switzerland	19
Portugal	17
Argentina	16
Israel	16
Japan	14
Russian Federation	14
Czech Republic	12
Germany	12
Italy	12
Slovak Republic	12
Romania	10
China	4
Scotland	2
Scotland	1
Scotland	1
Scotland	1

Exhibit 4.13   cont.

Population 3

Country	No. of Breaks
Iceland	219
Norway	219
USA	174
Switzerland	146
Israel	131
Korea	130
Czech Republic	113
Slovak Republic	113
Spain	113
Singapore	79
Canada	68
Switzerland	66
Australia	65
Hong Kong	63
Australia	62
USA	59
Canada	54
Israel	52
Colombia	49
Lithuania	49
Russian Fed.	49
Romania	47
Canada	46
New Zealand	45
Hong Kong	44
New Zealand	36
Colombia	35
South Africa	35
Israel	34
Romania	34
Sweden	34
Australia	32
Hong Kong	32
Canada	25
Hungary	25
Cyprus	23
Bulgaria	22
Mexico	21
Iran	19
Iran	17
South Africa	16
Greece	13
Greece	8
Iran	8
Russian Fed.	5
Japan	4
Romania	4
Israel	2
Netherlands	1
Netherlands	1

mean. Israel had one textbook similar to that of the Netherlands and another with about twice as many breaks in the content flow. The cross-national average indicates that a typical topic or content theme recurs from two to three times over the whole book for Population 1 mathematics textbooks.

US mathematics textbooks for eighth graders had almost four times as many breaks in content themes as the average. Colombian and Swedish textbooks also had high numbers of such breaks. The textbooks of the Czech and Slovak Republics, Japan, the Russian Federation, and Germany among others all had many fewer breaks than the cross-national mean. Textbooks from Israel and the Netherlands had about half as many breaks as the cross-national mean while those from the Czech Republic and Japan had even fewer. Scotland has books designed to cover only one topic but these are like modules and several of them are used to represent a year's coverage.

The textbook from Norway exhibits the greatest number of breaks among textbooks for advanced mathematics students in their final year. (The most widely used textbook from Iceland for this population is a translation of the same Norwegian textbook.) The US textbook is second only to the Norwegian textbook. On the other hand the textbooks from the Netherlands are very focused with only one content strand per book. The textbook from the Czech Republic differs little from the average number of breaks in US textbooks for this population, with about twice as many breaks as the cross-national mean. Israeli textbooks vary considerably within that nation's sample.

Science

Exhibit 4.14 presents data on the numbers of content strands in each science textbook in the sample for all three populations. The mean number of breaks between content themes in science was considerably larger than for mathematics. The number of breaks was 54 for Population 1 textbooks (similar to mathematics). The number of breaks was close to 95 both for Population 2 textbooks and for advanced physics textbooks which is almost twice as many breaks in these two populations' textbooks as in the corresponding mathematics textbooks.

The number of content strand breaks in US textbooks far exceeds the cross-national mean for Population 1 textbooks. In fact, there are almost four times as many breaks. The textbooks from Spain, Latvia and Romania also have a high number of breaks and are closest to the US books. Textbooks from Japan, Korea and Hong Kong are very different. Even combining the dual volume set in Japan they contain half as many breaks as the mean.

The number of content breaks in textbooks is higher for most countries at eighth grade. US textbooks again show an extreme number of such breaks, more than five times as many as the average across all books. One textbook from Australia approaches the number of breaks in US textbooks, as does one from Switzerland. One Hungarian textbook has close to the mean number of breaks, one has approximately three times that number, and two have substantially fewer. This suggests considerable within-country variation in the case of Hungary.

Norway exhibits an equivalently mixed picture. One Norwegian textbook has about three times as many breaks as the average but another has approximately half as many. Japanese eighth grade textbooks are extremely different from those of other countries. Instead of the number of breaks increasing from Population 1 to Population 2 they remain the same or even decrease. This results in eighth grade books that have less than half as many content strand breaks as the international average for Population 2 textbooks.

The advanced physics textbook with the largest number of breaks comes from Switzerland, with Bulgaria, Canada, and the US having textbooks that have very similar numbers of breaks. In fact three Swiss textbooks share this characteristic. In Norway this population's textbook has somewhat less than twice the number of breaks as the cross-national average. Hong Kong and Japanese textbooks have half as many breaks as the average as does one Canadian book.

Exhibit 4.14   Number of Strands or Breaks in Science Textbooks

Population 1

Country	No. of Breaks
USA	240
USA	240
Latvia	150
USA	145
Romania	139
Spain	135
Bulgaria	120
China	119
Spain	106
Canada	84
Hungary	84
Mexico	83
Slovenia	81
Czech Republic	76
Slovak Republic	76
China	72
Norway	71
Australia	67
Canada	67
Dominican Republic	63
Italy	59
Israel	58
Netherlands	58
Mexico	52
Colombia	50
France	48
Hong Kong	44
Austria	43
Colombia	42
South Africa	40
Ireland	38
Denmark	37
Ireland	34
Italy	34
Portugal	32
Israel	31
Russian Federation	30
Greece	29
South Africa	29
Hong Kong	22
Cyprus	19
Iceland	19
Italy	19
Iran	17
Czech Republic	16
Philippines	16
Canada	15
Japan	14
Australia	13
Korea	12
Japan	10
Japan	10
Singapore	10
Switzerland	10
Japan	9
Austria	8
Korea	7
Hong Kong	6
Hong Kong	4
South Africa	3

Population 2

Country	No. of Breaks
USA	633
USA	494
Switzerland	404
Australia	345
USA	342
Hungary	333
Norway	326
Spain	311
Canada	288
Romania	261
Italy	250
Slovenia	236
Austria	234
Bulgaria	217
Romania	217
China	208
Slovenia	204
China	190
Canada	188
Switzerland	163
Switzerland	156
Germany	148
Bulgaria	143
Spain	141
Sweden	130
Switzerland	130
Philippines	125
Canada	123
Cyprus	121
Portugal	118
Ireland	111
Mexico	109
Australia	107
Hungary	103
Austria	100
France	95
Sweden	95
Hungary	93
Portugal	91
Bulgaria	89
Czech Rep.	89
Slovak Rep.	89
Korea	88
Switzerland	87
Netherlands	84
Portugal	83
Colombia	82
Tunisia	82
Denmark	81
Netherlands	80
Hong Kong	77
Latvia	77
Mexico	77
Greece	67
Netherlands	67
Colombia	66
South Africa	65
Mexico	62
Canada	61
Mexico	60

Exhibit 4.14   cont.

Population 2 cont.

Country	No. of Breaks
Scotland	60
Argentina	58
Iran	58
Israel	58
New Zealand	57
Greece	56
Lithuania	56
Romania	56
Russian Fed.	56
Greece	54
Norway	54
China	52
Hong Kong	52
Cyprus	46
Germany	46
Dominican Rep.	44
Israel	44
Singapore	44
Cyprus	40
Iceland	40
Netherlands	39
Netherlands	38
Netherlands	37
Czech Rep.	35
Greece	35
Slovak Rep.	35
Argentina	33
Hong Kong	33
Netherlands	32
China	31
Czech Rep.	31
Hungary	31
Slovak Rep.	31
South Africa	31
New Zealand	29
Lithuania	26
Russian Fed.	26
Iceland	23
Slovenia	18
Iceland	17
Switzerland	15
Iceland	13
Iceland	13
South Africa	12
Netherlands	10
France	9
Germany	8
Germany	8
South Africa	8
Japan	6
Denmark	5
Japan	5
Russian Fed.	5
Japan	3
Japan	3
Japan	1
Japan	1
Japan	1
Japan	1
Lithuania	1

Population 3

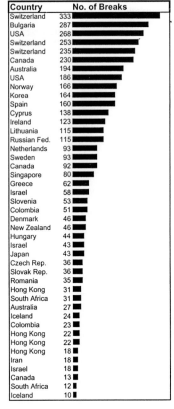

Country	No. of Breaks
Switzerland	333
Bulgaria	287
USA	268
Switzerland	253
Switzerland	235
Canada	230
Australia	194
USA	186
Norway	166
Korea	164
Spain	160
Cyprus	138
Ireland	123
Lithuania	115
Russian Fed.	115
Netherlands	93
Sweden	93
Canada	92
Singapore	80
Greece	62
Israel	58
Slovenia	53
Colombia	51
Denmark	46
New Zealand	46
Hungary	44
Israel	43
Japan	43
Czech Rep.	36
Slovak Rep.	36
Romania	35
Hong Kong	31
South Africa	31
Australia	27
Iceland	24
Colombia	23
Hong Kong	22
Hong Kong	22
Hong Kong	18
Iran	18
Israel	18
Canada	13
South Africa	12
Iceland	10

One way to understand a textbook structure laden with content strand breaks is to consider this as a degree of compositional complexity. Textbooks with more than one strand must coordinate a number of distinct content elements into a presentation that makes sense to teachers and students. Textbooks with greater numbers of strands appear to be attempting to incorporate many more distinct elements. The challenges for sense making would seem greater. As this number becomes even larger, exceeding the number of topics in the book, this results in even greater compositional complexity. In the case of the US it is striking to note that textbooks for Populations 1 and 2 appear to be extremely complex compared to other TIMSS countries' textbooks, while in Population 3, the US textbooks are much less complex than is typical. We are, of course, referring to structural complexity rather than the substantive complexity of the content.

COMPLEXITY IN THE PRESENTATION OF CONTENT

Complexity can also be the result of the type of representations used to convey the content strands in a textbook. Textbook authors may choose to present school mathematics and science through representations that do not make use of associations or applications to situations or events with which students are familiar. Such abstract representations represent a different type of cognitive complexity than representations that link mathematics and science ideas to particular and recognizable objects and events in students' lives. Students must primarily apprehend content through their mental faculties in the case of abstract representations. Concrete representations expressly relate to the world that student's experience through their senses as well as their minds.

The TIMSS' curriculum analysis procedures included determining the cognitive demands of the prevailing presentation style in each of a textbook's lessons. Coders registered to what extent the textbook used presentation strategies that relied on abstract representations or on concrete representations. Exhibit 4.15 summarizes the general patterns in textbooks in mathematics and science, intended for the different populations.

As a general pattern, almost one third of Population 1 mathematics textbooks are mostly made up of lessons that primarily use an abstract presentation strategy. That is, one third of this population's textbook sample is made up of textbooks that have 90 per cent or more of their lessons with content presented primarily through text and symbols. Approximately one half of the textbooks have 50 percent or more of their lessons presented in this abstract style. This strong TIMSS-wide tendency of preference for abstract presentation is further apparent in observing that almost 40 percent of Population 1 textbooks have no lessons that primarily use a concrete, pictorial presentation style.

This primacy of the abstract over the concrete increases in Population 2 textbooks and in textbooks intended for advanced mathematics students in their final year. The percentage of textbooks with no primarily concrete lessons increases to 50 percent in Population 2 and to almost three fourths for advanced mathematics textbooks. The percentage of textbooks having one half or more of their lessons primarily abstract increases to 65 per cent in Population 2 and 75 per cent for advanced mathematics.

School science textbooks are very different in Populations 1 and 2. In Population 1 textbooks, only approximately 20 percent of the textbooks have half or more of their lessons presented abstractly. This is a marked contrast to mathematics. The figure rises to one closer to that for mathematics in Population 2. About one half of the textbooks have one half or more of their lessons presented abstractly. However, textbooks for advanced physics students, are virtually identical to those for advanced mathematics students in this regard.

In this chapter various features related to the form and style of textbook coverage of content were discussed. Large variations were noted

Exhibit 4.15 Textbook Lesson Characteristics

	Percent of Lessons in Textbook	The Lesson in Mathematics Textbook is Primarily		The Lesson in Science Textbook is Primarily	
		Concrete & Pictorial	Textual & Symbolic	Concrete & Pictorial	Textual & Symbolic
Population 1	None	38	20	33	48
	<10%	14	6	10	16
	10-20%	8	6	8	8
	20-30%	7	6	5	3
	30-40%	6	6	5	3
	40-50%	3	4	0	2
	50-60%	4	7	0	0
	60-70%	1	4	2	5
	70-80%	0	4	3	0
	80-90%	3	6	5	10
	>90%	15	32	30	7
Population 2	None	49	14	30	22
	<10%	25	1	13	13
	10-20%	11	3	10	4
	20-30%	4	7	4	4
	30-40%	1	1	7	3
	40-50%	3	4	2	4
	50-60%	0	4	3	2
	60-70%	1	8	3	6
	70-80%	1	1	3	5
	80-90%	1	10	5	12
	>90%	3	46	20	24
Population 3	None	74	6	68	5
	<10%	10	4	20	5
	10-20%	2	2	2	7
	20-30%	0	4	0	0
	30-40%	0	2	0	2
	40-50%	4	6	2	7
	50-60%	4	4	2	0
	60-70%	0	4	0	0
	70-80%	4	0	0	9
	80-90%	2	8	0	7
	>90%	0	60	5	59

across countries. Certainly the potential exists for these features to either facilitate or be detrimental to the learning of the content contained in these books. In this way we continue to argue for our hypothesis that form and style are as critical to the development of content learning in textbooks as they are to the development of the theme in good literature.

Notes:

[1] A textbook strand is a sequence of contiguous blocks that have in common at least one code from the content aspect of the TIMSS mathematics or science framework. See the treatment of 'blocks' in Chapter 2 and Appendix A for an explanation of the TIMSS frameworks.

[2] See Chapter 2 for the definition of student populations for the TIMSS curriculum analysis.

[3] Schmidt et al., 1997a; Schmidt, McKnight, Valverde, Houang, & Wiley, 1997b; Schmidt, Raizen, Britton, Bianchi, & Wolfe, 1997c.

Chapter 5

Textbook Expectations for Performance

Textbooks not only put forward the content students are to learn but they also advocate what students should be able to do with that content. Textbook developers do not intend to simply convey information, but to encourage behaviors on the part of students. This book is about the structure and pedagogy of textbooks by which they do so. Chapters 2, 3 and 4 examine aspects of structure while this chapter has more direct implications for pedagogy and style.

We believe how content is presented in textbooks (with what expectations for performance) is how it will likely be taught in the classroom. We argued that the textbook characteristics described in Chapters 3 and 4 are inextricably tied to content and impact on the likelihood that such content will be learned. Performance expectations are similarly intertwined not with content generally but with content-specific pedagogy. As such we hypothesize that performance expectations embedded in textbooks will have an impact on what students are likely able to do with that content.

At the most basic level, textbooks are written with the expectation that students and their teachers will read and understand the content presented. However, textbook authors also aspire to elicit more complex performances from students. This is especially true as educational systems across the world pursue reform associated with the quest for higher achievement standards in school subjects highly valued by society. Consequently, another important dimension of textbooks examined in TIMSS were the demands they make on students' abilities, that is, the kinds of "performances" students would be expected to carry out as a result of mastering textbook content.

Textbooks can be more or less demanding of students in what they are required to be able to do with the content they learn. Some textbooks may emphasize students' abilities to read and recall information. Another may require students to perform complex operations with information – operations such as generating solution strategies or specifying possible outcomes resulting from an experiment before it is actually performed. These expectations regarding what students are required to do with content have been given various labels in the US including 'purposes', 'habits of mind' and 'abilities'.[1]

In the language of TIMSS, they are termed 'performance expectations' and are intended to measure the types of things students are intended to do with science or mathematics content. However, since the curriculum measurement methods for TIMSS were designed for implementation in a large-scale cross-national setting, such expectations could not be defined in terms of positing specific mental processes that might be involved in producing such performances. Identifying specific cognitive processes would be highly inferential, particularly subject to cultural differences, and likely pose insoluble challenges to obtaining acceptable levels of inter-rater reliability.

Thus, performance expectations in TIMSS refer simply to task expectations and demands put forth in a text that require comparatively low inferences to be identified on the part of coders. For mathematics there were a number of categories of performance expectations: knowing, using routine procedures, investigating and problem solving, mathematical reasoning, and communicating. For science there were also organizing categories: understanding; theorizing, analyzing, and solving problems; using tools, routine procedures, and science processes; investigating the natural world; and communicating. Within these broad organizing categories, the TIMSS curriculum frameworks identify a number of more specific behaviors.

For example, in mathematics the general category of investigating and problem solving[2] is made up of five specific behaviors. These are formulating and clarifying of problems and situations, developing a data-gathering or problem-solving strategy, executing some known or ad hoc solution strategy, predicting or specifying outcomes of operations before performing them, and finally, verifying or determining the correctness of results. The analysis of behaviors such as these as promoted in textbooks uncovered a variety of distinctive patterns in the performance demands in different countries. Exhibit 5.1 presents each broad performance expectation

Exhibit 5.1   Six Categories of Performance Expectations for Mathematics and Science

Mathematics Category	TIMSS Framework Code
1 Knowing & Using Vocabulary	Representing Recognizing equivalents Recalling mathematical objects & properties Using vocabulary & notation
2 Using Equipment/Performing Routine Procedures	Using equipment Performing routine procedures
3 Using Complex Procedures	Using more complex procedures
4 Investigating & problem solving	Formulating & clarifying problems & situations Developing strategy Solving Predicting Verifying
5 Mathematical reasoning	Developing notation & vocabulary Developing algorithms Generalizing Conjecturing Justifying & proving Axiomatizing
6 Complex Communication	Relating representations Describing/discussing Critiquing

Science Category	TIMSS Framework Code
1 Understanding Simple information	Simple information
2 Understanding Complex information	Complex information Thematic information
3 Theorizing, analyzing, & solving problems	Abstracting & deducing scientific principles Applying scientific principles to solve quantitative problems Applying scientific principles to develop explanations Constructing, interpreting, & applying models Making decisions
4 Using tools, routine procedures, & science processes	Using apparatus, equipment, & computers Conducting routine experimental operations Gathering data Organizing & representing data Interpreting data
5 Investigating the natural world	Identifying questions to investigate Designing investigations Conducting investigations Interpreting investigational data Formulating conclusions from investigational data
6 Communication	Accessing & processing information Sharing information

category in mathematics and science and the specific performance expectations of which they are comprised.

TEXTBOOK COVERAGE AS A WHOLE

We begin by first considering textbook coverage holistically. We examine performance expectations across countries without looking for characteristic national patterns.

Mathematics

Exhibit 5.2 presents the general results across the textbooks of all TIMSS countries at each of the grade levels studied. Clearly, without regard to the specific age for which mathematics textbooks were intended, the most common expectation for student performance was that they read and understand, recognize or recall or that they use individual mathematical notations, facts or objects. This is followed, again at each of the grade levels by the use of routine mathematical procedures. Most mathematics textbooks across the TIMSS countries included little else in terms of the more complex expectation types outlined in Exhibit 5.1.

Science

The same pattern holds for the science textbooks. The most common expectation was that pupils read and understand simple information. However, this was more true of textbooks intended for Populations 1 and 2, than for physics students in the final year of secondary school. More complex performance expectations rarely were present in even as little as one quarter of the fourth and eighth grade textbooks.

Physics textbooks present a less clear pattern. Most included a smattering of material (rarely more than five per cent) in which students

Exhibit 5.2   Distributions for the Performance Expectation Categories

	Percent Coverage in Mathematics Textbook	Mathematics Performance Expectation Categories					
		Knowing & Using Vocabulary	Using Equipment/Performing Routine Procedures	Using Complex Procedures	Investigating & problem solving	Mathematical reasoning	Complex Communication
Population 1	None	3	3	20	4	24	24
	<10%	4	10	54	41	53	61
	10-20%	3	1	16	29	17	9
	20-30%	7	14	7	10	1	6
	30-40%	17[a]	30	3	11	3	0
	40-50%	19	16	0	4	1	0
	50-60%	24	13	0	0	0	0
	60-70%	13	7	0	0	0	0
	70-80%	6	4	0	0	0	0
	80-90%	3	1	0	0	0	0
	>90%	1	0	0	0	0	0
Population 2	None	0	4	19	10	13	24
	<10%	3	11	60	26	44	57
	10-20%	4	13	11	28	15	11
	20-30%	15	18	10	10	8	6
	30-40%	15	26	0	13	13	3
	40-50%	24	19	0	6	4	0
	50-60%	24	7	0	4	0	0
	60-70%	14	1	0	3	3	0
	70-80%	0	0	0	1	0	0
	80-90%	0	0	0	0	0	0
	>90%	1	0	0	0	0	0
Population 3	None	2	14	30	4	6	18
	<10%	12	36	42	28	32	46
	10-20%	0	8	22	26	26	18
	20-30%	6	10	4	18	10	16
	30-40%	16	12	2	14	14	0
	40-50%	20	14	0	4	0	2
	50-60%	14	2	0	0	4	0
	60-70%	10	2	0	4	0	0
	70-80%	18	2	0	2	2	0
	80-90%	0	0	0	0	6	0
	>90%	2	0	0	0	0	0

[a] This figure should be interpreted as 17 percent of the Population 1 Mathematics textbooks have between 30 and 40 percent of the book coded as "knowing and using vocabulary."

were expected to investigate the natural world and communicate science ideas. Somewhat more emphasis was placed on requiring students to use laboratory and other tools in routine operations. Around 25 percent of the textbooks had 30 percent or more of the book covering material where the performance expectations advocated were more complex requiring the students to theorize, analyze or solve problems. Understanding simple information was emphasized much less than in textbooks intended for younger pupils, and much less than was the case for mathematics textbooks intended even for students studying advanced mathematics in their final year of secondary school.

LESSON COVERAGE

The focus in this section is on a textbook lesson and the set of expectations for student performance that it tries to elicit. Expectations regarding performances for textbook lessons were occasionally not of a single type. It was sometimes necessary to indicate more than one performance expectation to characterize a lesson or part of a lesson. That is, within the context of a lesson, textbooks sometimes intended to elicit a number of different performances from students. More variety in the type of performance expectations within a lesson suggests an intention that students not only acquire knowledge and skills but also that they be required to use the knowledge and skills of the lesson in a number of different ways. Exhibit 5.3 gives the percentage of textbooks at each of the TIMSS populations that had at least one lesson in which a more complex combination of expectations were present, i.e., where multiple codes were necessary to capture the performance expectations of at least one lesson in the textbook. Certainly, simple one-code lessons were the most prevalent across textbooks in both mathematics and science and at all populations.

Exhibit 5.3   Combinations of Performance Expectation Categories in Lessons

Combinations of Performace Expectation Categories in Mathematics Textbooks

Number of Performance Expectation Categories	Knowing & Using Vocabulary	Using Equipment/ Performing Routine Procedures	Using Complex Procedures	Investigating & problem solving	Mathematical reasoning	Complex Communication	Percent of Textbooks with this Combination in at least one Lesson		
							Population 1	Population 2	Population 3
None									
One Category	✓						▰▰▱	▰▰▱	▰▰▱
		✓					▰▰▱	▰▰▱	▰▰▱
			✓				▰▰▱	▰▰▱	▰▰▱
				✓			▰▰▱	▰▰▱	▰▰▱
					✓		▰▱▱	▰▰▱	▰▰▱
						✓	▰▱▱	▰▱▱	▰▱▱
Two Categories	✓	✓					▰▰▱	▰▰▱	▰▱▱
	✓		✓				▰▱▱	▰▱▱	▰▱▱
	✓			✓			▰▱▱	▰▰▱	▰▱▱
	✓				✓		▰▱▱	▰▱▱	▰▱▱
	✓					✓	▰▱▱	▰▱▱	▰▱▱
		✓	✓				▰▱▱	▰▱▱	▰▱▱
		✓		✓			▰▱▱	▰▰▱	▰▱▱
		✓			✓		▰▱▱	▰▱▱	▰▱▱
		✓				✓	▰▱▱	▰▱▱	▰▱▱
			✓	✓			▰▱▱	▰▱▱	▰▱▱
			✓		✓				▰▱▱
			✓			✓	▰▱▱	▰▱▱	▱▱▱
				✓	✓		▰▱▱	▰▰▱	▰▱▱
				✓		✓	▰▱▱	▰▱▱	▰▱▱
					✓	✓		▰▱▱	▰▱▱
Three Categories	✓	✓	✓					▰▱▱	▰▱▱
	✓	✓		✓			▰▱▱	▰▱▱	▰▱▱
	✓		✓	✓					▰▱▱
	✓		✓		✓				▰▱▱
	✓			✓		✓			▰▱▱
	✓				✓	✓			▰▱▱
		✓	✓	✓					▰▱▱
		✓	✓		✓				▰▱▱
		✓		✓	✓				▰▱▱
		✓		✓		✓		▰▱▱	▰▱▱
				✓	✓	✓			▰▱▱

Exhibit 5.3   cont.

Combinations of Performace Expectation Categories in Science Textbooks

Understanding Simple information	Understanding Complex information	Theorizing, analyzing, & solving problems	Using tools, routine procedures, & science processes	Investigating the natural world	Communication	Percent of Textbooks with this Combination in at least one Lesson		
						Population 1	Population 2	Population 3
						▪☐		▪☐
✓						▪▪	▪▪	▪▪
	✓					▪☐	▪☐	▪☐
		✓				▪☐	▪☐	▪▪
			✓			▪☐	▪☐	▪☐
				✓		▪☐	▪☐	▪☐
					✓	▪☐	▪☐	▪☐
✓	✓					▪☐	▪☐	▪☐
✓		✓					▪☐	▪☐
✓			✓			▪☐		
✓				✓				
✓					✓			
	✓	✓					▪☐	▪☐
	✓		✓			▪☐	▪☐	
	✓			✓				
	✓				✓			
		✓	✓				▪☐	▪☐
		✓		✓				▪☐
		✓			✓		▪☐	
			✓	✓			▪☐	
			✓		✓			
				✓	✓	▪☐		
✓	✓	✓						
✓	✓		✓					
✓		✓	✓					
✓		✓		✓				
✓			✓		✓			
✓				✓	✓			
	✓	✓	✓					▪☐
	✓	✓		✓				
	✓		✓	✓				
	✓		✓		✓			
			✓	✓	✓			

Legend:

☐	10%
▪☐	20%
▪☐	30%
▪☐	40%
▪☐	50%
▪☐	60%
▪☐	70%
▪☐	80%
▪▪	90%
▪▪	100%

Science

In science, well over 90 per cent of the countries' textbooks at all three grade levels had some lessons with only the expectation that students would read and understand simple information.

More than one expectation in the same lesson was much less common. One common pattern of this type in science included the use of tools, routine procedures or scientific processes in lessons in which students were also required to read and understand either simple or complex information. This was especially the case for textbooks intended for Population 1. All lessons with other types of combinations of performance expectations were somewhat rare in Population 1.

For eighth grade textbooks, multiple performance expectation (PEs) lessons were found in a higher percent of the textbooks. The most prevalent was the combination of understanding complex or thematic information and theorizing, analyzing and solving problems found in around one-quarter of all Population 2 books. Several other combinations were found to be present in from 10 to 20 percent of the eighth grade books.

Physics textbooks for secondary school students were similar to eighth grade books on this characteristic. The combination of PEs that was the most prevalent at eighth grade was also the most prevalent for the physics books (27 percent).

Mathematics

The combination of different performance expectations within one lesson was more common in mathematics. Simple single-expectation lessons were still the most common across TIMSS mathematics textbooks. Almost half of the textbooks intended for fourth graders had lessons in which students were intended to read and understand simple facts, and use vocabulary and notation as well as to perform routine mathematical procedures. More than one fourth of the textbooks intended for this age group had lessons that either combined routine mathematical procedures with investigating and problem solving, or with using more complex mathematical procedures.

Similarly, mathematics textbooks intended for thirteen-year-olds had lessons that combined various performance expectations more frequently than in science books. In the case of textbooks intended for advanced mathematics students in the final year of secondary school, the frequency of such combinations of performance expectations was lower but still occurred in over one fourth of the textbooks.

HANDS-ON EXPERIENCES

Several types of performance expectations in school science are of particular interest given current trends in science education reform around the world. These include expectations that have students solve problems and participate in scientific processes that involve investigating the natural world. Exhibit 5.4 shows the frequency with which lessons in TIMSS textbooks included expectations of this type.

It is notable that these types of performance expectations occurred very infrequently across the TIMSS textbooks. At least half of the textbooks devoted zero percent to these types of expectations in both Populations 1 and 2. In fact, in Population 1 over 60 percent did not include most of these expectations. The story is somewhat different for Population 3 but even here most of the textbooks devoted 5 percent or less to these types of expectations.

A small fraction of the TIMSS countries included expectations in 15 percent or more of their textbooks that nine-year-old students would

Exhibit 5.4   Distributions of the Percent of Select Performance Expectations for Science Textbooks

| | | Percent of Science Textbooks with Each Performance Expectation | | | | | | | | | |
| | Percent of Each Textbook containing the Particular Performance Expectation | Theorizing, analyzing, & solving problems | | | | | Investigating the natural world | | | | |
		Abstracting & deducing scientific principles	Applying scientific principles to solve quantitative problems	Applying scientific principles to develop explanations	Constructing, interpreting, & applying models	Making decisions	Identifying questions to investigate	Designing investigations	Conducting investigations	Interpreting investigational data	Formulating conclusions from investigational data
Population 1	None	70	85	59	62	69	66	67	49	64	64
	<10%	30	15	41	38	29	26	30	38	34	34
	10-20%	0	0	0	0	2	0	3	12	2	2
	20-30%	0	0	0	0	0	5	0	2	0	0
	30-40%	0	0	0	0	0	0	0	0	0	0
	40-50%	0	0	0	0	0	3	0	0	0	0
Population 2	None	55	39	45	50	62	67	65	45	63	63
	<10%	40	55	51	44	36	33	35	47	35	36
	10-20%	2	5	3	4	0	1	0	8	2	1
	20-30%	3	0	0	2	2	0	0	1	0	0
	30-40%	0	1	1	0	0	0	0	0	0	0
	40-50%	0	0	0	0	0	0	0	0	0	0
Population 3	None	27	5	16	32	66	77	82	57	75	77
	<10%	64	34	77	61	34	23	18	41	25	23
	10-20%	7	36	7	0	0	0	0	0	0	0
	20-30%	2	21	0	7	0	0	0	2	0	0
	30-40%	0	2	0	0	0	0	0	0	0	0
	40-50%	0	2	0	0	0	0	0	0	0	0
	50-60%	0	0	0	0	0	0	0	0	0	0
All Populations	None	54	45	43	50	65	68	69	48	66	66
	<10%	42	40	53	46	34	29	30	43	33	33
	10-20%	2	10	3	2	0	0	1	7	1	1
	20-30%	2	4	0	2	1	1	0	1	0	0
	30-40%	0	1	0	0	0	0	0	0	0	0
	40-50%	0	0	0	0	0	1	0	0	0	0
	50-60%	0	0	0	0	0	0	0	0	0	0

be involved in identifying questions to investigate or to actually conduct investigations. The relative lack of such expectations is seen in science textbooks at the other grade levels as well. Closer inspection of the textbooks in each country showed very few textbooks deviating from the TIMSS-wide comparative lack of emphasis on these "hands-on science" expectations. Population 3 textbooks included somewhat more material related to students' solving quantitative problems but not in the actual conducting or designing of investigations.

Reform movements in school mathematics have typically called for an emphasis on investigation and problem solving in addition to mathematical reasoning. However, Exhibit 5.5 shows that the situation regarding the presence of reform orientations in mathematics textbooks was little different from that found for science textbooks. This was especially true for mathematics reasoning but there were exceptions for problem solving. For both Populations 2 and 3 a higher percentage of textbooks had expectations dealing with the solving of problems but even here this material was less than a third of the book. For eighth grade, 51 percent of the books contained 10% or more of the content with this expectation. The corresponding number for the advanced mathematics textbooks was 56 percent.

Generally we found that science textbooks more than mathematics textbooks are likely to present students with textual material that does not intend that they engage in more than one performance expectation in each lesson. In both mathematics and science it appears that key elements of suggested reforms are not widely incorporated in school textbooks, at least at the time that the TIMSS sample of textbooks was drawn. This again is more true for science.

It is apparent that the analysis of the presence of performance expectations in the TIMSS textbooks presents an interesting paradox. At a time in which school mathematics and science are deemed by many

Exhibit 5.5 Distributions of the Percent of Select Performance Expectations for Mathematics Textbooks

Percent of Each Textbook containing the Particular Performance Expectation	Percent of Mathematics Textbooks with Each Performance Expectation										
	Investigating & problem solving					Mathematical reasoning					
	Formulating & clarifying problems & situations	Developing strategy	Solving	Predicting	Verifying	Developing notation & vocabulary	Developing algorithms	Generalizing	Conjecturing	Justifying & proving	Axiomatizing
Population 1											
None	17	33	10	49	50	50	51	54	54	60	93
<10%	70	61	72	51	44	41	43	46	43	39	7
10-20%	6	6	10	0	6	9	3	0	3	1	0
20-30%	3	0	6	0	0	0	1	0	0	0	0
30-40%	3	0	1	0	0	0	1	0	0	0	0
40-50%	1	0	1	0	0	0	0	0	0	0	0
50-60%	0	0	0	0	0	0	0	0	0	0	0
Population 2											
None	24	28	10	29	25	38	40	26	33	26	69
<10%	58	63	39	71	67	51	51	68	60	63	31
10-20%	14	7	28	0	8	10	3	6	4	7	0
20-30%	3	1	10	0	0	1	1	0	3	3	0
30-40%	1	1	8	0	0	0	1	0	0	1	0
40-50%	0	0	3	0	0	0	1	0	0	0	0
50-60%	0	0	3	0	0	0	1	0	0	0	0
Population 3											
None	20	18	10	46	34	40	30	30	36	18	72
<10%	68	68	34	54	62	52	56	58	56	50	26
10-20%	6	10	42	0	4	8	4	4	2	12	2
20-30%	2	2	8	0	0	0	2	4	0	12	0
30-40%	2	0	0	0	0	0	4	2	0	4	0
40-50%	2	2	4	0	0	0	0	2	0	0	0
50-60%	0	0	2	0	0	0	4	0	4	2	0
60-70%	0	0	0	0	0	0	0	0	2	2	0
All Populations											
None	20	27	10	41	37	43	42	38	42	37	79
<10%	65	64	50	59	57	48	50	57	53	51	21
10-20%	9	7	25	0	6	9	3	3	3	6	1
20-30%	3	1	8	0	0	1	2	1	1	4	0
30-40%	2	1	4	0	0	0	2	1	0	2	0
40-50%	1	1	3	0	0	0	1	1	0	0	0
50-60%	0	0	2	0	0	0	2	0	1	1	0
60-70%	0	0	0	0	0	0	0	0	1	1	0

countries to be among the most socially valued curricular areas (for example, as demonstrated by the number of countries that participated in TIMSS) the most prevalent expectations for student performance promoted by textbooks were remarkably basic and comparatively undemanding. Most textbooks attempted little more than to promote the reading and understanding of factual information as well as the continued practice of routine skills.

This finding seems simple and straightforward. Its importance is substantial. The paucity of complex expectations for student performance in textbooks suggests the difficulty in enacting many of the reform visions of school mathematics and science meant to be distinct improvements over prevailing instructional practices. If textbooks shape the probability of classroom implementation of pedagogical activities and help determine what is likely and what is not, then the textbooks examined in this study suggest that serious reform at the classroom level is unlikely. Such reform, either in mathematics or science, would require a drastic change in the complexity of the performance expectations found in textbooks.

NOTES:

[1] National Council of Teachers of Mathematics, 1989; Project 2061 - American Association for the Advancement of Science, 1993; and National Research Council, 1996 respectively.

[2] Framework code 2.3 – see Appendix B.

Chapter 6

Textbook Lessons

Textbooks are made up of lessons. Metaphorically the macrostructure that we examined in Chapter 3 is the "skeleton" that defines a textbook. If so, then examined more closely – microscopically – the "bones" of that skeleton also have structure that helps determine their role in the structure and function of the whole. What we see in this closer look we will term the "microstructure" of textbooks and it is the subject of this chapter.

The units primarily used in the content analysis of textbooks were defined to be *lessons*. A lesson was identified as a segment of text material devoted to a single main mathematical or scientific topic, and intended to correspond to a teacher's classroom lesson on that topic taught over one to three instructional periods.[1]

Using lessons provides an alternative way of gauging differences in the length of textbook material – one that focuses on length as descriptive of the fine structure of textbooks. Lessons require textbook space. They take up pages and parts of pages. Different lessons use pages in different ways as they cover different contents. Differences in the number of pages intended for coverage within a lesson tells us more about how textbooks are structured.

Exhibit 6.1 shows the number of pages per lesson in mathematics and science textbooks according to the student population for which the textbook was intended. An increase in the average number of pages for an instructional lesson can be observed in both subject areas as the grade level of the textbook increases. In mathematics the successive increase in page length of lessons progressed from a mean of four pages per lesson in Population 1 textbooks to about six pages for textbooks intended for

Exhibit 6.1   Distribution of Average Number of Pages Per Lesson

	Population	Number of Textbooks	Average Number of Pages per Lesson	Standard Deviation	Minimum	Maximum	Distribution
Mathematics Textbooks	1	71	3.7	2.2	1.1	11.2	
	2	71	5.1	3.7	1.5	23.6	
	3	47	5.5	3.4	1.3	21.1	
Science Textbooks	1	59	3.7	2.1	1.6	16.5	
	2	119	4.8	3.5	1.3	21.5	
	3	43	5.0	3.7	1.2	19.3	

mathematics specialists in the final year of secondary school. In science there was an analogous increase in average length as units are intended for progressively older students. More interestingly, some textbooks have very long lessons ranging from 10 to 20 pages in length. These are, however, clearly exceptions as 50 percent of all textbooks at each population fell in the range of three to six pages per lesson. The reasons for textbooks with longer lessons are not known but could include a different interpretation of what a lesson is.

THE RHETORIC OF TEXTBOOK LESSONS

Lessons are designed by textbook authors to influence students directly through contact with the book's printed page. Lessons are also designed to influence students indirectly by influencing teachers' usage of instructional time. Thus, they are best understood as having been designed as instruments for persuasion. They are intended to influence the actions of the protagonists of educational systems – students and teachers. To influence these actors, lessons can be structured in a variety of ways. "Rhetoric," since classical times, has been the term for the study of the use of symbols and words in an effort to influence human action and thought. We are thus interested in the rhetoric of textbooks as persuasive instruments that potentially shape classroom practice and educational opportunity.

Textbooks vary in the preponderance and length of the different rhetorical elements that make up lessons. The textbook has been divided into *blocks*. These blocks are nested within lessons and, indeed, the very name "blocks" was meant to suggest their role as the building blocks of the larger structures of lessons. In the TIMSS methodology these blocks were classified according to whether they constituted narrative or graphical elements; exercise or questions sets; worked examples; or activities. These block types are the basic components that define the rhetoric of textbooks – the elements put together to carry out strategies of persuasion.

Narrative elements are perhaps the easiest elements to identify in textbooks. They use sentences and paragraphs to explain concepts and topics through description and discussion. They tell stories and state facts and principles through narration. Activity elements (termed 'activity blocks' in the TIMSS measurement methodology) are segments of the textbooks that contain instructions and suggestions for student activities. Often they contain instruction for the conduct of some sort of 'hands-on' experience. This might include an experiment in science or collecting and using data in mathematics.

A narrative element requires children to interact with textbooks in a fairly traditional manner. For narration the book provides the total intended educational experience. Activity elements, on the other hand, point beyond the book to the world. They prescribe a set of actions that students are intended to perform outside of the world of the textbook and these actions are intended to constitute a part of their educational experience. In narration, all referents are internal and inherently static, they require only that students be readers. Whether students read actively or passively, whether they make connections and make sense, is largely a function of the individual reader and his or her motivation. Only secondarily is it a function of that which is read. In contrast, activities prescribe an intended dynamic use of the textbooks and inherently demand an active learner.

Exercises and question sets – another block type – also engage students more actively than narrative blocks. These provide instructions and opportunities to practice and acquire particular skills. They are similar to activity blocks in requiring that students engage in performances that are different from reading and understanding. They are similar to narrative blocks in that the exercises provide all that is necessary for the pedagogical experience. However, exercises and question sets unlike activity blocks do not direct students to the world outside of textbooks, except as these are parts of the internalized world of students.

Another block type, called 'worked examples' refers to material that details the execution of a particular algorithm or solution strategy through an illustration with detailed annotation and description. These blocks are similar to narrative blocks in that the material in these is intended for students to read and understand. They differ in that they are structured by the pursuit of an answer to a problem or question and presuppose that students will follow the flow of that pursuit.

DECLARATIVE SCIENCE, APPLIED MATHEMATICS

Given the above definitions we first examine the contrast between narrative and activity oriented blocks (including both types – 'activities' and 'exercise and question sets'). This provides an overall characterization of the textbooks as to whether they are mostly declarative or activity-oriented.

We first look at the proportion of textbook space devoted to three types of rhetorical elements.

Exhibit 6.2 presents the data for mathematics textbooks. In mathematics, we can see that textbooks across all populations were mostly made up of exercises and question sets. In fact, the typical percent of textbook space allocated is between 50 and 60 percent for Populations 1 and 2. In Population 3, the typical percent is lower – 35 percent – but there is a larger emphasis on worked examples. Mathematics textbooks intend students to engage in a great deal of skill practice. It is also important to note that the typical amount of narrative in the mathematics textbooks increased over the three grade levels as does the inclusion of worked examples. The amount of textbook space allocated to activities decreased over the three grade levels.

The case of science is very different as Exhibit 6.3 shows. From this table it is clear that narration was the primary vehicle for the conduct of lessons as depicted in science textbooks regardless of the grade-level. Narration typically accounted for around 70 percent of the science textbooks.

COUNTRY DIFFERENCES IN THE USE OF RHETORICAL ELEMENTS

We have characterized mathematics and science textbooks for the three populations without looking for characteristic rhetorical differences among the TIMSS countries. We now turn to examining country differences. Exhibits 6.4 and 6.5 display the prevalence of the four types of rhetorical elements for both mathematics and science and for each country textbook in the sample.

Exhibit 6.2   Distribution of Different Block Types in Mathematics Textbooks

	Block Types	Percent of Textbooks without such element	Average Percent of Blocks[a]	Standard Deviation	Minimum	Maximum	Distribution
Population 1 (72 Textbooks)	Narrative & Related Graphic	1%	24%	13%	1%	62%	
	Exercises/ Question Set	0%	59%	16%	20%	94%	
	Activities	18%	5%	4%	1%	17%	
	Worked Examples	6%	11%	7%	1%	35%	
Population 2 (72 Textbooks)	Narrative & Related Graphic	0%	31%	14%	8%	81%	
	Exercises/ Question Set	0%	52%	18%	11%	86%	
	Activities	51%	2%	2%	1%	9%	
	Worked Examples	4%	12%	7%	1%	34%	
Population 3 (50 Textbooks)	Narrative & Related Graphic	0%	42%	14%	17%	75%	
	Exercises/ Question Set	0%	36%	18%	5%	70%	
	Activities	88%	2%	3%	1%	7%	
	Worked Examples	0%	19%	8%	3%	46%	

[a] Statistics in this exhibit and Exhibit 6.3 are computed over those textbooks in which the rhetorical element is present. For example, when present, 24% of the blocks are narrative and related graphic on average for Population 1 Mathematics textbooks.

Mathematics

Here we see that individual textbooks in the TIMSS sample vary appreciably on all four types of rhetorical elements. The proportion of narrative and exercise blocks in mathematics textbooks was similar across Populations 1 and 2 as shown in Exhibit 6.3. However, narrative and graphics elements were almost entirely absent in the fourth grade textbooks of some countries. This was the case, for example, for textbooks from

Exhibit 6.3   Distribution of Different Block Types in Science Textbooks

	Block Types	Percent of Textbooks without such element	Average Percent of Blocks [a]	Standard Deviation	Minimum	Maximum	Distribution
Population 1 (60 Textbooks)	Narrative & Related Graphic	0%	65%	14%	28%	100%	
	Exercises/ Question Set	8%	18%	12%	2%	49%	
	Activities	5%	15%	10%	2%	44%	
	Worked Examples	83%	3%	2%	1%	9%	
Population 2 (120 Textbooks)	Narrative & Related Graphic	0%	72%	13%	44%	100%	
	Exercises/ Question Set	8%	16%	10%	1%	48%	
	Activities	18%	10%	7%	1%	32%	
	Worked Examples	58%	3%	3%	1%	18%	
Population 3 (44 Textbooks)	Narrative & Related Graphic	0%	73%	12%	45%	99%	
	Exercises/ Question Set	5%	18%	11%	1%	42%	
	Activities	52%	5%	4%	1%	20%	
	Worked Examples	7%	6%	4%	1%	18%	

[a]See footnote in Exhibit 6.2.

Argentina (which actually had no narrative blocks), Switzerland, and the Netherlands. Switzerland also had one textbook at eighth grade that effectively had no narrative blocks. By contrast the lowest percent of narrative blocks in Population 3 belonged to a Dutch textbook (17 percent). On the other hand, narrative blocks were extremely predominant (three fourths or more of the book) for the Romanian and Bulgarian eighth grade textbooks.

Exhibit 6.4   Composition of Rhetorical Elements in Mathematics Textbooks

Population 1

Country	Narrative & Related Graphic	Exercises/ Question Set	Activities	Worked Examples
Switzerland	2%	94%	1%	2%
Denmark	7%	93%	0%	0%
Switzerland	3%	91%	1%	4%
Korea	4%	90%	3%	3%
Netherlands	1%	88%	2%	0%
Austria	10%	85%	2%	3%
Greece	7%	84%	1%	8%
Portugal	3%	82%	3%	10%
Korea	8%	81%	5%	6%
Norway	13%	79%	4%	3%
Austria	19%	74%	4%	3%
USA	17%	73%	4%	5%
Norway	13%	72%	5%	7%
New Zealand	9%	71%	6%	12%
USA	15%	70%	4%	9%
USA	20%	68%	4%	8%
Israel	20%	67%	5%	7%
Ireland	24%	67%	1%	8%
Cyprus	6%	67%	9%	18%
Cyprus	3%	65%	10%	20%
Israel	22%	65%	0%	13%
Argentina	0%	65%	0%	35%
Singapore	21%	64%	2%	13%
Singapore	23%	64%	1%	11%
Philippines	26%	64%	1%	9%
Canada	19%	63%	2%	14%
Japan	36%	63%	1%	0%
Japan	33%	63%	0%	1%
Romania	21%	62%	9%	8%
Slovenia	25%	62%	2%	11%
China	26%	62%	0%	9%
Switzerland	22%	62%	4%	7%
Hungary	23%	61%	7%	3%
USA	19%	61%	3%	13%
Japan	34%	60%	4%	2%
Iceland	15%	60%	9%	16%
South Africa	27%	60%	11%	2%
Mexico	31%	59%	10%	0%
Korea	22%	59%	5%	15%
Canada	33%	58%	4%	3%
Japan	37%	57%	2%	1%
France	22%	57%	1%	9%
Dominican Republic	38%	56%	0%	3%
Ireland	26%	55%	1%	19%
Canada	29%	55%	1%	16%
Australia	16%	54%	17%	12%
Israel	32%	54%	6%	9%
Colombia	33%	51%	10%	4%
China	32%	51%	0%	12%
Canada	32%	51%	4%	5%
Iceland	33%	51%	9%	7%
Thailand	35%	51%	1%	13%
Colombia	18%	49%	7%	16%
Bulgaria	24%	49%	1%	24%
Hong Kong	23%	48%	10%	19%
Hong Kong	27%	45%	6%	18%
Russian Federation	9%	45%	0%	3%
Korea	34%	44%	8%	15%
Hong Kong	27%	43%	7%	22%
South Africa	28%	42%	8%	22%
Italy	49%	42%	0%	9%
Italy	42%	40%	0%	17%
Scotland	40%	39%	2%	10%
Australia	37%	39%	10%	14%
Argentina	28%	38%	0%	34%
Hong Kong	30%	37%	5%	29%
Spain	52%	36%	0%	7%
Iran	34%	35%	8%	17%
Latvia	16%	34%	13%	4%
Czech Republic	50%	32%	3%	13%
Slovak Republic	50%	32%	3%	13%
Spain	62%	20%	0%	11%

Population 2

Country	Narrative & Related Graphic	Exercises/ Question Set	Activities	Worked Examples
Switzerland	8%	86%	0%	6%
Switzerland	12%	85%	2%	0%
Switzerland	11%	79%	5%	4%
Sweden	11%	78%	0%	8%
Dominican Republic	19%	77%	0%	4%
USA	15%	75%	3%	8%
Tunisia	24%	73%	1%	0%
Czech Republic	12%	72%	0%	15%
Slovak Republic	12%	72%	0%	15%
Israel	15%	72%	0%	12%
USA	20%	72%	1%	5%
Israel	15%	71%	1%	3%
China	19%	69%	0%	12%
Netherlands	25%	69%	1%	3%
Italy	31%	68%	0%	1%
Austria	18%	68%	1%	9%
Israel	29%	68%	0%	2%
Switzerland	19%	67%	2%	10%
Canada	25%	66%	0%	8%
Cyprus	26%	66%	0%	9%
USA	20%	65%	3%	8%
Singapore	20%	63%	2%	15%
Switzerland	26%	62%	1%	10%
Netherlands	30%	61%	0%	4%
New Zealand	12%	59%	5%	23%
Czech Republic	19%	59%	0%	22%
Slovak Republic	19%	59%	0%	22%
Thailand	27%	59%	2%	11%
Argentina	34%	58%	0%	8%
USA	25%	58%	2%	12%
Mexico	29%	58%	1%	13%
Iran	33%	58%	3%	1%
Sweden	34%	57%	3%	3%
Norway	35%	57%	0%	4%
Portugal	11%	57%	6%	14%
Ireland	29%	56%	0%	14%
Denmark	32%	56%	5%	5%
Canada	26%	55%	2%	12%
Iceland	31%	55%	0%	12%
USA	30%	54%	0%	16%
Netherlands	38%	52%	0%	7%
Japan	38%	50%	2%	9%
Philippines	35%	49%	2%	14%
Greece	32%	48%	0%	17%
France	32%	48%	1%	9%
South Africa	33%	47%	2%	15%
Scotland	43%	46%	0%	11%
Romania	28%	46%	4%	22%
Australia	43%	45%	0%	11%
Slovenia	42%	45%	1%	12%
Colombia	31%	44%	9%	15%
Japan	46%	44%	1%	8%
Italy	40%	44%	6%	10%
Korea	34%	43%	2%	13%
Scotland	42%	42%	0%	8%
Scotland	44%	39%	4%	12%
Austria	57%	37%	0%	0%
Colombia	41%	35%	2%	14%
Hong Kong	40%	34%	1%	23%
China	61%	33%	0%	7%
Hungary	29%	30%	0%	12%
South Africa	46%	29%	1%	23%
Scotland	32%	29%	0%	25%
Russian Federation	34%	28%	0%	9%
Spain	42%	28%	0%	28%
Russian Federation	34%	26%	0%	19%
Germany	37%	25%	0%	10%
Bulgaria	43%	19%	0%	28%
Spain	39%	17%	0%	34%
Romania	81%	15%	0%	4%
Germany	62%	12%	0%	27%
Bulgaria	75%	11%	0%	9%

Exhibit 6.4   cont.

Population 3

Country	Narrative & Related Graphic	Exercises/ Question Set	Activities	Worked Examples
Netherlands	17%	70%	0%	11%
Netherlands	29%	66%	0%	3%
South Africa	25%	65%	1%	10%
Canada	25%	61%	0%	14%
Mexico	21%	60%	3%	15%
Israel	26%	58%	0%	15%
New Zealand	21%	58%	0%	17%
Canada	31%	55%	0%	14%
Canada	20%	55%	0%	25%
Lithuania	32%	55%	0%	14%
Russian Federation	32%	55%	0%	14%
Switzerland	38%	52%	0%	9%
Australia	38%	50%	0%	10%
Canada	38%	48%	1%	13%
Cyprus	31%	48%	0%	21%
New Zealand	28%	47%	0%	22%
Israel	33%	46%	0%	20%
Korea	32%	46%	0%	23%
Colombia	31%	45%	0%	16%
Israel	39%	45%	0%	14%
Switzerland	44%	43%	0%	13%
USA	39%	42%	0%	18%
Greece	39%	41%	0%	20%
Greece	37%	38%	0%	24%
South Africa	43%	38%	0%	19%
Romania	51%	36%	0%	13%
Japan	48%	34%	0%	17%
Sweden	45%	33%	0%	21%
USA	50%	33%	0%	15%
Singapore	50%	32%	0%	19%
Australia	48%	30%	0%	22%
Romania	37%	29%	7%	27%
Australia	43%	26%	0%	30%
Colombia	39%	26%	0%	17%
Hong Kong	41%	26%	1%	32%
Hong Kong	52%	21%	0%	27%
Czech Republic	58%	20%	0%	20%
Slovak Republic	58%	20%	0%	20%
Romania	58%	18%	0%	25%
Hungary	75%	17%	0%	8%
Russian Federation	44%	17%	0%	7%
Iceland	56%	13%	0%	31%
Norway	56%	13%	0%	31%
Israel	67%	13%	0%	21%
Bulgaria	59%	12%	1%	23%
Iran	49%	10%	0%	40%
Spain	61%	9%	0%	23%
Iran	71%	7%	0%	14%
Iran	70%	6%	0%	24%
Hong Kong	33%	5%	0%	46%

Worked examples were common elements across textbooks but generally constituted less than a fifth of the book, yet their use varied from no such blocks in some eighth grade textbooks from Austria, Tunisia, and Switzerland to 34 percent of the blocks in one textbook from Spain. For advanced mathematics textbooks this ranged from around zero (the Netherlands – 3 percent) to almost half of the book (Hong Kong – 46 percent). Further, although the use of exercise sets was common in mathematics textbooks at all populations, Swiss eighth grade textbooks were almost entirely composed of exercises (62 to 86 percent). For fourth grade, the proportion of two Swiss books devoted to exercises exceeded 90 percent.

Science

Narrative and graphic blocks were much more common in science textbooks, as Exhibit 6.5 illustrates. Even here the range across individual textbooks was large for all three grade levels extending from around a third of the book to the whole book. Textbooks from Iceland relied heavily on such blocks across the three populations.

Despite exceptions such as textbooks from the Netherlands (eighth grade), Japan, Austria and Portugal (fourth grade), narrative blocks were the most predominant type (around half of the book or more) across the TIMSS science textbook sample. Activity blocks were uncommon in Population 3 but more common in Population 1. Their inclusion in fourth grade textbooks was the most variable ranging from no such blocks to almost half of the blocks in a book. The latter was a book from Cyprus.

From this table it is clear that the rhetorical basis of mathematics and science lessons is very different. Most commonly, mathematics textbooks pursued the application of mathematical knowledge and skill through the extensive use of exercises and question sets. On the other hand science textbooks took a declarative approach regarding skills and knowledge, conveying these through methods that are predominantly narrative. This is clearly illustrated in the scatter plot found in Exhibit 6.6.

There is a generally negative relationship between the inclusion of narrative blocks and the inclusion of problems or exercise sets in a textbook. This implies that a textbook with more narrative blocks has in general fewer exercises or problem sets. Fourth and eighth grade mathematics textbooks are all mostly located in one region of the graph (more exercise sets and fewer narrative blocks). On the other hand, science textbooks intended for the same grade levels are located in a different region of the graph indicating large numbers of narrative blocks but fewer exercises. The

Exhibit 6.5   Composition of Rhetorical Elements in Science Textbooks

Population 1

Country	Narrative & Related Graphic	Exercises / Question Set	Activities	Worked Examples
Iceland	100%	0%	0%	0%
Denmark	95%	2%	3%	0%
Italy	86%	11%	2%	0%
Iran	86%	4%	11%	0%
Italy	85%	4%	7%	0%
USA	85%	7%	8%	0%
Latvia	80%	2%	15%	0%
Romania	80%	8%	10%	3%
Bulgaria	79%	21%	0%	0%
Colombia	78%	5%	15%	0%
Slovenia	78%	11%	10%	1%
Mexico	76%	3%	20%	0%
Czech_Republic	74%	15%	8%	0%
Slovak_Republic	74%	15%	8%	0%
South_Africa	74%	4%	21%	0%
South_Africa	73%	8%	17%	0%
Korea	72%	0%	27%	0%
USA	72%	13%	8%	0%
Korea	72%	0%	28%	0%
Canada	72%	15%	11%	0%
Spain	72%	13%	6%	0%
Canada	72%	16%	12%	0%
Switzerland	72%	19%	2%	2%
South_Africa	71%	15%	14%	0%
Canada	70%	11%	16%	0%
Israel	69%	5%	14%	0%
Australia	68%	0%	20%	0%
Hong_Kong	67%	27%	6%	0%
Mexico	66%	19%	12%	0%
Greece	66%	30%	5%	0%
Italy	64%	17%	18%	1%
France	63%	25%	11%	0%
Philippines	63%	23%	12%	0%
Ireland	62%	14%	25%	0%
China	62%	19%	20%	0%
USA	61%	24%	7%	0%
China	61%	16%	23%	0%
Austria	60%	35%	2%	0%
Spain	58%	25%	7%	0%
Dominican_Republic	58%	34%	8%	0%
Ireland	57%	28%	15%	0%
Netherlands	57%	36%	7%	0%
Colombia	55%	4%	38%	0%
Russian_Federation	54%	27%	15%	0%
Hungary	53%	25%	19%	0%
Hong_Kong	53%	34%	10%	3%
Australia	52%	0%	37%	0%
Japan	52%	11%	22%	9%
Singapore	52%	33%	14%	0%
Norway	51%	5%	6%	0%
Japan	51%	12%	26%	4%
Czech_Republic	50%	49%	0%	0%
Cyprus	50%	6%	44%	0%
Hong_Kong	47%	30%	23%	0%
Hong_Kong	47%	33%	16%	4%
Japan	47%	7%	39%	3%
Israel	46%	7%	6%	0%
Japan	42%	11%	38%	5%
Austria	36%	46%	17%	0%
Portugal	28%	37%	19%	0%

Population 2

Country	Narrative & Related Graphic	Exercises / Question Set	Activities	Worked Examples
Sweden	100%	0%	0%	0%
Switzerland	97%	0%	0%	0%
Switzerland	97%	0%	0%	0%
Switzerland	97%	0%	3%	0%
Iceland	96%	4%	0%	0%
Slovenia	94%	0%	6%	0%
Greece	93%	6%	0%	1%
Iceland	93%	7%	0%	0%
Iceland	92%	8%	0%	0%
China	90%	8%	1%	0%
Portugal	90%	0%	0%	0%
Portugal	90%	0%	4%	0%
Tunisia	90%	7%	2%	0%
Czech_Republic	90%	0%	0%	6%
Slovak_Republic	90%	0%	0%	6%
China	89%	10%	1%	0%
Bulgaria	88%	12%	0%	0%
Romania	87%	4%	6%	2%
Hong_Kong	86%	10%	3%	0%
Romania	86%	4%	10%	0%
Hungary	85%	14%	1%	0%
Czech_Republic	84%	12%	3%	0%
Slovak_Republic	84%	12%	3%	0%
Greece	83%	14%	0%	1%
Greece	83%	9%	3%	0%
Italy	83%	12%	4%	1%
Iran	82%	10%	7%	1%
Denmark	82%	2%	8%	0%
China	81%	15%	4%	0%
Japan	81%	12%	6%	0%
South_Africa	81%	2%	5%	1%
Mexico	81%	9%	10%	0%
Hong_Kong	81%	11%	5%	0%
Mexico	80%	2%	15%	3%
Hungary	80%	11%	7%	0%
Bulgaria	80%	18%	0%	2%
Cyprus	80%	10%	7%	0%
Iceland	80%	21%	0%	0%
Netherlands	80%	8%	5%	0%
Argentina	79%	4%	5%	11%
Hong_Kong	79%	2%	18%	0%
Scotland	79%	11%	8%	0%
Colombia	79%	16%	5%	0%
Slovenia	78%	7%	9%	0%
Argentina	77%	3%	17%	0%
Korea	77%	5%	17%	1%
South_Africa	77%	9%	3%	0%
South_Africa	76%	5%	18%	1%
Germany	75%	15%	8%	3%
Latvia	74%	5%	1%	18%
USA	74%	20%	3%	0%
Cyprus	74%	8%	11%	1%
Greece	74%	16%	0%	0%
South_Africa	74%	8%	17%	1%
Switzerland	74%	0%	0%	0%
USA	74%	15%	7%	0%
Iceland	74%	6%	19%	1%
Netherlands	73%	20%	4%	0%
Germany	73%	22%	4%	0%
Bulgaria	73%	20%	0%	4%
Japan	73%	5%	22%	0%
Ireland	72%	12%	10%	3%
Lithuania	72%	21%	5%	0%
Russian_Federation	72%	21%	5%	0%
Hungary	71%	18%	8%	0%
Norway	70%	1%	11%	0%
Mexico	70%	16%	6%	7%
Slovenia	70%	13%	15%	0%
Germany	70%	16%	0%	0%
Canada	70%	25%	5%	0%
Israel	68%	10%	7%	0%
Austria	68%	28%	1%	0%
Hungary	68%	8%	20%	2%
China	68%	22%	7%	3%
Israel	67%	8%	17%	1%
Canada	67%	21%	11%	0%
Switzerland	66%	14%	14%	1%
Cyprus	66%	14%	17%	1%
Japan	66%	8%	18%	2%
Norway	66%	7%	0%	0%
Netherlands	65%	24%	0%	0%
Mexico	64%	17%	19%	0%
Canada	64%	21%	14%	0%
Japan	63%	11%	21%	1%
Japan	63%	12%	6%	1%
Germany	63%	1%	32%	0%
Lithuania	63%	15%	6%	3%
Russian_Federation	63%	15%	6%	3%
Japan	62%	10%	24%	1%
Romania	62%	32%	6%	0%
Singapore	62%	8%	28%	1%
Japan	62%	16%	9%	2%
Japan	61%	26%	6%	0%
USA	61%	18%	5%	1%
Dominican_Republic	61%	24%	15%	0%
Spain	61%	19%	3%	0%
Denmark	61%	10%	24%	5%
Portugal	60%	33%	3%	0%
Australia	59%	32%	7%	1%
Philippines	58%	29%	11%	0%
Switzerland	58%	38%	2%	1%
Lithuania	56%	31%	7%	2%
Russian_Federation	56%	31%	7%	2%
New_Zealand	55%	31%	14%	0%
Netherlands	55%	32%	10%	0%
Czech_Republic	54%	23%	20%	2%
Slovak_Republic	54%	23%	20%	2%
Austria	54%	24%	12%	9%
France	54%	45%	1%	0%
Canada	54%	20%	11%	0%
Colombia	52%	28%	17%	0%
Australia	51%	13%	11%	0%
Netherlands	51%	30%	5%	5%
Spain	51%	33%	2%	1%
Netherlands	50%	28%	8%	0%
France	50%	19%	21%	1%
New_Zealand	48%	32%	20%	1%
Sweden	44%	35%	9%	0%
Netherlands	44%	48%	0%	0%
Netherlands	44%	26%	10%	1%

Population 3

Country	Narrative & Related Graphic	Exercises / Question Set	Activities	Worked Examples
Hong_Kong	99%	0%	0%	2%
Hong_Kong	95%	1%	0%	4%
Iceland	93%	1%	0%	3%
Australia	91%	2%	0%	3%
Hong_Kong	91%	0%	0%	9%
Australia	89%	5%	0%	5%
Hong_Kong	89%	12%	0%	0%
Bulgaria	83%	11%	0%	0%
Iceland	82%	2%	0%	17%
Hungary	80%	17%	0%	3%
Lithuania	79%	12%	1%	2%
Russian_Federation	79%	12%	1%	2%
Slovenia	78%	7%	1%	13%
Ireland	76%	11%	5%	7%
Singapore	75%	18%	0%	7%
Romania	75%	18%	0%	7%
Canada	75%	13%	4%	7%
Cyprus	75%	10%	3%	11%
Korea	74%	13%	8%	4%
Israel	74%	25%	0%	0%
Sweden	74%	23%	0%	1%
Iran	74%	16%	3%	7%
Canada	73%	13%	0%	14%
Israel	73%	23%	3%	1%
South_Africa	73%	15%	4%	8%
USA	73%	8%	0%	18%
Japan	72%	23%	2%	3%
Norway	71%	17%	0%	11%
Israel	71%	22%	5%	2%
USA	71%	20%	2%	3%
Czech_Republic	69%	12%	2%	1%
Slovak_Republic	69%	12%	2%	1%
Netherlands	68%	21%	5%	2%
Switzerland	68%	9%	20%	1%
Colombia	63%	12%	3%	7%
South_Africa	62%	23%	9%	5%
Denmark	61%	27%	7%	5%
Colombia	61%	20%	10%	7%
Greece	59%	34%	0%	5%
Spain	53%	33%	0%	9%
Canada	52%	42%	0%	4%
Switzerland	49%	39%	0%	5%
Switzerland	48%	40%	0%	4%
New_Zealand	45%	41%	0%	12%

Population 3 science textbooks are similar to the other science books but the corresponding advanced mathematics textbooks are spread out across the graph – spanning the two regions just described.

When countries participating in the TIMSS were surveyed in the early 1990s, most countries reported a number of reforms or managed changes underway in science education. In virtually all cases these reforms included stronger emphasis on experimentation and real-world inquiry. It is possible that the intention was that teachers were to use sources parallel to the textbooks in developing opportunities for students to engage in such a type of activity. However, it is yet notable that the textbooks themselves by and large do not provide many examples of this type of pedagogy. The US is a clear example. None of the most commonly used science textbooks intended for the US fourth or eighth grades contained more than 10 percent activity blocks. Physics textbooks that were intended for college-preparatory courses in the final year of secondary education contained virtually none. Given our conjecture that how content is presented in textbooks is likely how it will be taught in the classroom from a pedagogical point of view, these data imply difficulty in the implementation of such reforms.

What can explain this preponderance of narration in a world that seems to emphasize the importance of more "hands on" science? Why does science not at least make use of question sets as mathematics does? One possibility is that the predominance of narrative and graphics in science textbooks stems from presenting second-hand experience with the objects of science by "showing and telling" about phenomena as an (admittedly unsuitable) replacement for direct experience with those phenomena. This would have the convenience of restricting science instruction to the printed world of the textbook and not requiring the use of laboratory equipment or encounters with a wider variety of empirical phenomena. The latter would be more difficult especially in traditional classrooms. Alternatively, it may be that science textbooks were typically meant to be more widely supplemented than was the case for mathematics textbooks. Either of these explanations remains at best conjectural.

Across the world, there are many significant efforts to reform pedagogy in both mathematics and science. This is supported by the perception among policy makers that widespread knowledge in these areas contributes to the quality of the labor force of a country and as a result the competitiveness of the economy. The fact remains that most mathematics textbooks were concerned with the application of mathematics knowledge to exercises and question sets to be solved entirely with reference to material contained in the textbook. Most science textbooks presented the bulk of the science curriculum in the form of material to be read and understood. One possible implication of this is that classroom instruction in mathematics

Exhibit 6.6   Scatter Plot of Narrative versus Exercises Blocks

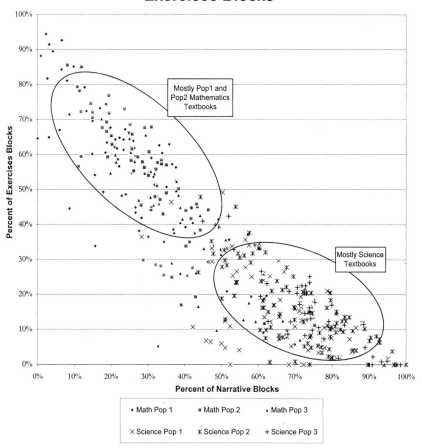

would mostly be about doing exercises and in science it would mostly be about reading or listening. At least that would be the implication of our hypothesis about the impact of the structure and pedagogy of textbooks on classroom instruction.

The argument to be made for the reform of science and mathematics education toward the inclusion of more first-hand experiences with real world data is based on a belief that such experience is qualitatively superior to second-hand or contrived experiences conveyed by words and pictures and by self-referential questions. Attempting such mathematics and science reform while ignoring the pedagogical nature of the textbooks appears at best to be a policy worth reconsidering and at worst to be catastrophically foolish.

NOTES:

[1] Detailed treatment of the techniques of this component of TIMSS can be found in: Schmidt, McKnight, Valverde, Houang, & Wiley, 1997b; Schmidt, Raizen, Britton, Bianchi, & Wolfe, 1997c; Survey of Mathematics and Science Opportunities, 1992a; Survey of Mathematics and Science Opportunities, 1992b; Survey of Mathematics and Science Opportunities, 1993.

Chapter 7

A Holistic View of Textbooks

In the preceding chapters, we have examined a set of characteristics that describe textbook structure and pedagogy to help understand how textbooks from across the world vary on these dimensions. Previous work has established that these same books differ in their content profiles. The hypothesis here is that form and style are potentially important in that they can influence the degree to which the content profile is taught by teachers and learned by students.

We began by examining variation in physical characteristics such as the number of pages, the total surface area of pages and the amount of graphics. Review of those features reveals that countries across the world challenge their students with pedagogical tools that are physically dissimilar. Some countries provide students with such quantities of reading material that the majority of instructional time might conceivably (depending on how textbooks are used) be made up of attempting to follow each of the pedagogical strategies and situations proposed in the book. In other countries textbooks do not attempt to compete for such significant portions of teachers' time or their students' time. They clearly envision classrooms in which textbook use is but one of many activities.

The analyses have also pointed out the varied ways in which textbooks intend instruction in mathematics and science to unfold over the course of a year. Some books pursue a few themes in depth with varied expectations for student performance. Other books have many brief themes that occur sporadically, even randomly, throughout the textbook. These structures are likely to promote distinct types of learning opportunities in classrooms.

Further we have seen that most textbooks attempt to convey a set of content objectives fairly similar to those most other countries propose for the same grade level although differing in emphasis. Some provide their mathematics and science students with textbooks that are quite unique in their content coverage.

Textbooks also differ in the types of behaviors they attempt to elicit from students. These differences seem more significant to classroom pedagogy, which also has an impact on opportunities to learn. Most textbooks do not go very far beyond providing material for reading and practicing routine operations. The lessons that textbooks offer as models of valid techniques for accomplishing pedagogical goals are also extremely wide-ranging in form and structure. All of these features are likely to promote learning in distinctive ways.

For the purpose of characterizing the variation in textbooks, each structural and pedagogical feature has been examined by itself. However, there remains an inescapable aspect of all of this that must be taken into account – what is used in the classroom and hence likely affects student opportunities to learn is a single entity. However useful it is for analytical purposes to break down textbooks into a number of identifiable attributes, they are in fact pedagogical instruments that enter classrooms as wholes. Teachers and students use the book and as such approach its attributes simultaneously – or in such a rapidly concatenated succession – that it is useful to think of textbooks as possessing an overall structure made up of the multiple attributes simultaneously. It is in the final analysis that holistic experience that is related to opportunity to learn. As such we now turn to characterizing the variability of textbooks across the "TIMSS world" from the holistic perspective.

In Chapter 1, we introduced 12 variables representing each of the major types of textbook attributes that we then examined in detail in Chapters 2 through 6. As reported in that chapter, those representative variables proved powerful in distinguishing among textbooks. In Chapter 3, we discussed how textbooks holistically organize content, performance expectations, and rhetorical devices into an overall structure. This was based on a newly devised graphical display intended to summarize the manner in which some of these features unfold from the first to the last page of the textbook. In this chapter we address the overall structure of textbooks in a different way.

Analytically the question here is whether we can categorize textbooks – ignoring subject matter, grade level and country – by considering the 12 aspects simultaneously. Once categorized in this fashion, how many different types of textbooks are there and how many of each type are there? That is, do textbooks cluster into a small number of groups by sharing similarities and differences on these various attributes? If such clusters do in fact exist, are they related to grade level or subject matter? Are textbooks of the same subject or the same grade level similar in the structural and pedagogical characteristics? As will be seen, analyzing textbooks in this manner uncovers results that both reveal patterns that can be explained in light of current understandings and that also challenge us to think of textbooks as complex pedagogical and political tools.

DESIGN OF THE ANALYSES

The 12 variables used to characterize the textbooks for these analyses included four variables (as described in Chapter 6) related to the nature of the rhetoric – percent of textbook space devoted to exercises, activities, worked examples and a combined percentage of the textbook containing narrative and related graphics.

Measures of the form and style associated with content were also included. These included a measure of the number of topics that accounted for 80 per cent of the textbook, the number of textbook strands, and the total number of topics in the textbook. A measure of content uniqueness was also included – the percentage of the textbook that covers the mathematics or science content that is most commonly intended across the world.

The number of textbook pages represented the physical characteristics of the textbooks. A final group of three variables provided measures of expectations for student performance. The first was the percentage of the textbook that requires students to read and understand the written material. The second was a variable measuring the percentage of the textbook's blocks that requires students to engage in scientific theorization or mathematical problem solving. Third and finally was a variable that measured the percentage of the textbook's blocks that requires the student to engage in mathematical reasoning or in investigations of the natural world.

The statistical procedures used assume the textbooks could be represented in a multidimensional manner in which each dimension is a textbook attribute. The clustering procedure used first simplified the space and then pinpointed specific locations within this reduced space where different textbooks fell.[1] Hence, it uncovers groups of textbooks where similarity and difference are defined multidimensionally with reference to the 12 attributes considered simultaneously. This is a simplified way to represent textbook variability.

Two linear combinations (principal components) of the twelve variables accounted together for approximately fifty- percent of the variance in the 400 textbooks from forty-three countries considered in this analysis. Based on this, five types of textbooks were defined. The five groups contained 80, 70, 90, 104 and 56 textbooks respectively. In Exhibit 7.1 we present the means of the twelve variables for each of the five groups.

Exhibit 7.1   Means of the Twelve Textbook Characteristics for Each Type of Textbook

	Textbook Type				
	1	2	3	4	5
Percent of Textbooks in each Textbook Type*	20.0%	17.5%	22.5%	26.0%	14.0%
Percent of Each Textbook Type that are:					
Mathematics Textbooks	100.0%	21.4%	96.7%	1.9%	0.0%
Science Textbooks	0.0%	78.6%	3.3%	98.1%	100.0%
Total	100%	100%	100%	100%	100%
Percent of Each Textbook Type that are for:					
Population 1	40.0%	31.4%	35.6%	25.0%	26.8%
Population 2	28.8%	50.0%	41.1%	55.8%	57.1%
Population 3	31.3%	18.6%	23.3%	19.2%	16.1%
Total	100%	100%	100%	100%	100%
Textbook Characteristics:					
Average Percent of Narrative Materials	25.6%	58.7%	33.1%	72.7%	71.9%
Average Percent of Exercises and Questions Set	56.2%	23.9%	49.3%	13.3%	15.3%
Average Percent of Activities	1.8%	9.8%	2.3%	8.1%	7.0%
Average Percent of Worked Examples	14.0%	3.1%	12.1%	1.8%	1.4%
Average Percent of Performance Expectations for Understanding	43.9%	51.7%	48.2%	68.1%	67.1%
Average Percent of Performance Expectations for Problem Solving	24.9%	12.4%	12.3%	7.2%	6.0%
Average Percent of Performance Expectations for Reasoning	18.0%	8.7%	8.9%	3.2%	4.0%
Average number of Strands/Breaks	27.6	26.3	75.9	66.6	186.0
Average Number of Topics	15.9	14.0	22.7	21.8	42.4
Average Number of Topics needed to cover 80% of the Textbook	3.5	3.5	6.8	5.5	9.8
Average Number of Pages	210.2	155.9	349.1	196.9	331.2
Average Percent of relevant World Core Topics	100.0	91.6	79.1	77.0	76.2

* Four hundred textbooks were used in the analysis.

A Typology of Textbooks

Examination of the data shows that the TIMSS population from which the book was sampled is not strongly related to membership in the five clusters. That is, the books from the different populations spread themselves fairly evenly across the groups. This implies that when we are dealing with structural and pedagogical characteristics rather than specific content there is no unique elementary, middle, and high school textbook. The one exception is that there is a smaller percentage of books intended for Population 2 in Group 1, with a correspondingly larger percent of books intended for Population 3 in Group 1.

A typical book in Group 1 emphasizes exercises and problem sets heavily. It addresses a small number of topics and correspondingly is of moderate size with a quarter of the book having expectations for student performance that concern problem solving. This is more than is present in the typical textbook of the four other groups. These books are not complex thematically; there are only a small number of strands. These strands deal almost exclusively with topics that are commonly intended across the world ('world core' topics). There is a slightly higher percentage of books in this group that are intended for nine-year-olds. All are mathematics books. Since the nature of the content was not used as a criterion for clustering, this indicates a similarity in mathematics textbooks that is based on form and style rather than specific content. Clearly such structural and pedagogical features do differentiate mathematics from science textbooks to some extent since Group 1 is comprised of all mathematics textbooks.

Group 2 textbooks are small textbooks, with lessons presented mostly by narrative. They focus on a small number of topics the majority of which are commonly intended across the TIMSS nations. These books also contain a small number of themes. The textbook lessons mostly expect children to read and understand. There are both mathematics and science textbooks in this group.

Group 3 contains large books with many pages that cover a moderate array of topics with less focus than is common in the first two groups. There are many different fragmented content themes in these textbooks, with a large number of occasions when the textbook shifts attention from one set of topics, to an entirely new set (many breaks or strands). The lessons are mostly made up of exercises. Almost all of these textbooks cover mathematics. There are only three exceptions – a science textbook intended for Population 2 in the Netherlands and two science textbooks intended for Population 3 (one from New Zealand and another from Greece).

Group 4 textbooks heavily emphasize narrative and have both moderate breadth and depth, as well as a moderate number of pages. Most lessons have the simplest expectations for student performances. There are many thematic shifts and the textbooks are moderately aligned with the content expectations of the majority of TIMSS nations. All of the textbooks are for science with only two exceptions – mathematics textbooks intended for nine-year-olds in Norway and the US.

Books in Group 5 also place an emphasis on conveying science through narration. There are numerous topics addressed – almost twice as many or more than any other group which is accompanied by a lack of focus. These books are very large in terms of the number of pages and mostly have the simplest of expectations for student performance. These are books that are thematically very cumbersome – there are at least twice as many occasions in which these books abandon themes and begin new ones as in any other group. All of these are science textbooks that are moderately aligned with science topics commonly intended across the TIMSS countries. There is a slightly higher percentage of books intended for Population 2 here. The fact that this group is comprised totally of science textbooks again confirms that science and mathematics books not only differ in terms of their content but in terms of their form and style as well.

COUNTRY MEMBERSHIP IN THE TYPOLOGY

Our emphasis in this book is on individual textbooks and not country differences. However, after having performed the statistical clustering, we turn our attention briefly to the question of textbook structures that are characteristic of particular nation's textbooks.

We see some evidence of characteristic textbook structures that follow country patterns. In the case of the US, essentially all mathematics textbooks belong to Group 3 and all science textbooks to Group 5. This suggests homogenous approaches to school science and mathematics in the United States which is consistent across intended grade levels and across all publishers. The style and form seem even homogenous across subject matters since Group 3 is similar in structure and pedagogy to Group 5.

Similarly, most textbooks from Japan belong to Groups 1 or 2 while Cypriot mathematics textbooks all belong to Group 1, and all science textbooks to Group 4. However, such characteristic structures for a country's textbooks were relatively uncommon across the TIMSS sample. Most countries have textbooks with different structures. This is especially true for Hong Kong, the Netherlands, Singapore and Spain.

This finding is particularly striking in the case of the United States. The structural similarity of mathematics and science textbooks exists in a competitive textbook market with no national-level content standards or curriculum. Japan also has a free textbook market, but with tighter governance of the content of schooling guaranteed through an established national curriculum. Other countries with textbook markets (yet tighter governance than the US) such as France have textbooks with diverse structures. In Korea the situation is a bit more complex. Most mathematics textbooks (with one exception) belong to Group 1. Science textbooks in Korea are more structurally varied and belong to three different groups.

A GRAPHICAL REPRESENTATION OF TEXTBOOK VARIABILITY

Half of the variance in textbook structure and pedagogy can be explained by the two principal components associated with the twelve variables used in the analysis to form the textbook typology. In the preceding we used these components to form the five groups. Another way to look at the variability across textbooks is to plot the textbooks graphically. A complimentary set of important patterns emerge from this plot supporting the conclusions cited in the previous sections.

Exhibit 7.2 plots each textbook according to its value on each of the two principal components using different symbols to represent mathematics and science textbooks. Clearly, although content was not included in the analysis, mathematics and science textbooks across TIMSS countries are different not only in their content but in their form and style as well.

Exhibit 7.3 displays the same textbooks but using different symbols – symbols that indicate the population for which textbooks were intended. Here it is apparent that across the TIMSS countries there are no typical textbook structures that can be deemed characteristic of each of the three TIMSS populations separately. The graphs and their implications are consistent with the previous conclusions suggesting the lack of population differences but the presence of subject matter differences in textbooks.

Textbooks convey potential educational opportunities. They do so in characteristic ways. For example, science textbooks rely heavily on words and pictures while mathematics textbooks rely heavily on exercises and question sets. There are interesting regularities and interesting differences. Above all it is clear that how textbooks convey educational opportunities – how they bridge the chasm between the intentions of curricular policies and the realities of classroom implementations – is no simple matter. Structural and pedagogical characteristics do not uniquely identify textbooks for any

Exhibit 7.2   Textbooks Classified by Subject Matter

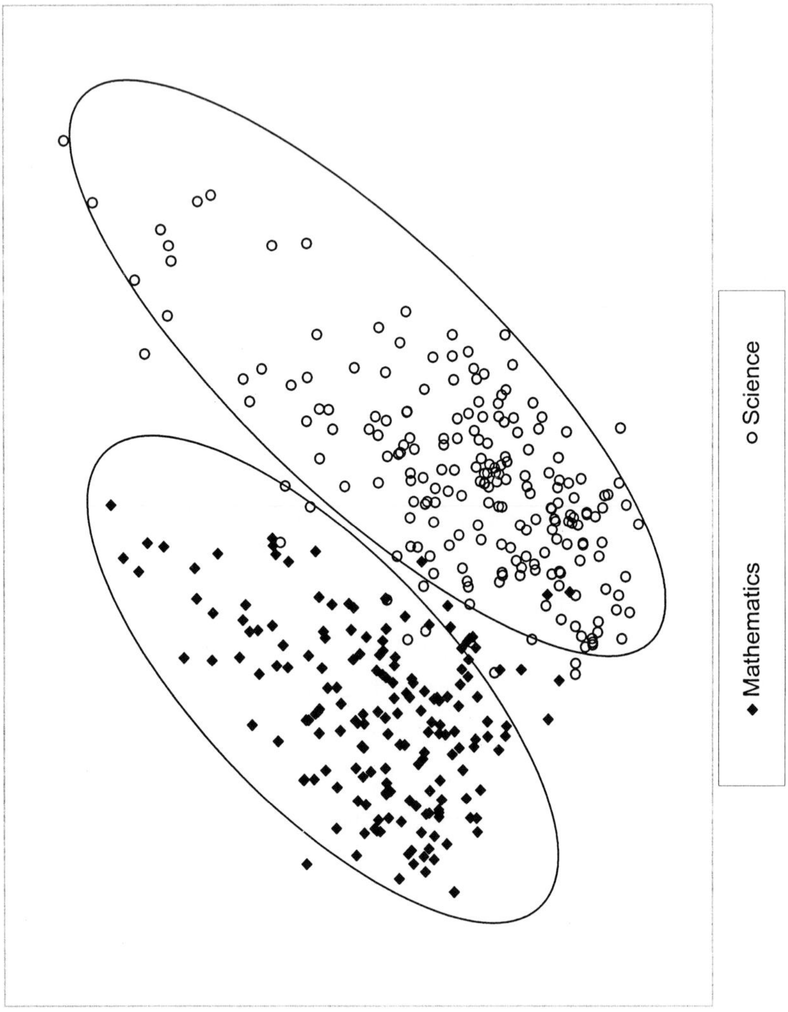

◆ Mathematics   ○ Science

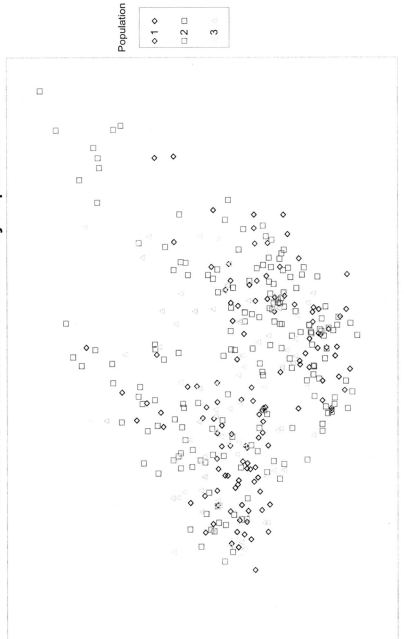

Exhibit 7.3   Textbooks Classified by Population

Population

◇ 1   □ 2   △ 3

population of students or for most countries. However, mathematics and science textbooks do differ in form and style as well as in the content they provide.

Notes:

[1] Exploratory principal components analysis was used to determine textbook groupings. Linear combinations of a number of variables were made in order to account for the maximum amount of variance.

Chapter 8
Translating Policy into Practice

The opportunities to learn experienced by students in classrooms around the world are the result of both cultural forces that permeate the society of which the educational system is a part, and of specific educational policies. Though mindful of the many forces affecting the results of their efforts, decision makers in educational systems are continuously confronted with the question of which educational opportunities are to be provided to which students, within constraints that are social, cultural, economic and political. Definition of these opportunities and the provisions for delivering them to students result from social and political processes of decision-making that vary from nation to nation. Resulting instruments – statements of content standards – detailing goals are necessarily also varied. However, all nations confront two fundamental challenges.

The first challenge is to delineate the desired educational outcomes that national schooling is intended to promote. The result is a fundamental definition of the purposes of schooling. Although there are a number of purposes commonly set forward across the world, in all TIMSS nations one such purpose is to master subject matter in mathematics and the sciences. All educational systems concern themselves with the need to provide guidance in this regard to those who participate in that educational system. A common policy instrument to accomplish this includes a system-wide statement of academic goals. Such statements may originate at one or more of various levels of the educational system, resulting from the work of national legislative bodies, national or subnational secretariats or ministries of education, other regional or municipal actors, school districts or individual schools. These statements might be called courses of study, content standards, or some other term. In any case they specify academic objectives. For example, they spell out which mathematics and science topics and skills students are intended to acquire in elementary and secondary school – by grade or cycles of grades.

The second challenge is how to cause the implementation of these standards. The instruments we term 'standards' here are but one element in the academic content of the governance of educational systems. These instruments differ considerably in how they are intended to contribute to governance. Some require compliance by actors in the system. Others intend to provide guidance by informing or persuading. A common feature of these instruments, regardless of the precise manner in which they are intended to govern, is that they establish goals without clearly identifying the concrete actions that must be taken to ensure delivery of the intended opportunities. In many cases systemic governance recognizes that there are many valid routes to enacting the vision of educational quality present in the standards. In other cases other instruments are intended to provide a specification of the officially sanctioned route to their enactment. In both cases the definitions of specific implementation strategies are left to other instruments and participants in the system.

If the shaping of educational opportunities can be seen to begin with the establishment of policy through content standards, clearly such standards require other systemic participants to interpret and translate them into concrete actions. Thus they require re-expression in terms of their use in classrooms. The textbook is a primary form of such re-expression. It is a form that has an impact on how other systemic actors, especially teachers and students, interpret the standards. Textbooks serve this function by design. In all cases they are intended to exemplify the type of concrete steps that can be taken to accomplish the stated content standards. In some countries these are books with extremely circumscribed roles. For example, some limit themselves to suggesting what constitutes valid ways to practice required skills. This is certainly the case of the exercise-oriented books that we have encountered in the TIMSS curriculum analysis.

However, in the majority of TIMSS countries, textbooks are more ambitious. They attempt to specify how classroom lessons can be structured. These specifications include an identification of the topics to be explored, their sequence, the activities that can be used in the exploration of the topic, and the behaviors that should be expected from students as part of this exploration. Thus, textbooks translate policy intentions into practice – into potential pedagogical implementation strategies. In the case of educational systems that are governed by the prescription of an official route to curriculum policy enactment, the text becomes the program of activities. In the case of educational systems that govern through informing or persuading, these textbook translations of system goals become important examples and primary instruments for persuasion.

In mediating between system goals and the realities of classrooms, textbooks are a critical factor in characterizing educational opportunities. Many educational system participants are concerned with establishing system goals. However, it is the primary professional responsibility of teachers to be concerned with their implementation. Understanding teachers' instructional behaviors is necessary to characterize educational opportunities. Understanding educational system elements that influence teacher and student behavior is critical as well.[1]

Textbooks are written to support and to guide classroom instruction. In this book we have attempted to characterize the type of guidance and support they provide. In previous work we have portrayed how the profile of content covered in textbooks varies across countries. We have also demonstrated that such variability is related to the variability in achievement gain or learning across countries. In the work reported here we have addressed how a textbook's structure and pedagogy also varies across textbooks and countries. Hence, we have characterized the models of classroom instruction that they intend as a referent for classroom teachers.

These models have proven varied in myriad ways. Physically, textbooks differ widely in size even when intended for students of the same age. More importantly, their macro and microstructures vary, as those embody the representation of the model of classroom instruction they promote. We conjecture that such textbook models are almost certainly related to how teachers actually teach the content in their classrooms.

In some countries textbooks promote the coverage of many different topics. As we have seen, this is sometimes done through a progression of successive themes, or in other cases through a number of themes occurring either simultaneously or in rapid succession. Each structure presents its own challenges to sense making. Textbooks also differ in the extent to which students are expected to center their learning in the world of the textbook itself or whether they are directed to the real world as they engage in learning. These differences also challenge students differently and are likely to promote different skills and different dispositions toward the subject matter and its role in students' lives. This is likely their intention. There is less variation in the behaviors that textbooks intend to be elicited from students. By far the majority of textbooks in the TIMSS curriculum study more than anything else intended children to read and to practice the skills that they read about – in both mathematics and science. These findings are important in a number of ways.

First, we have found substantial variation in the structure and pedagogy of textbooks as we have in terms of their content (as reported elsewhere). The content coverage of textbooks is related both to teacher coverage and to achievement gain. We argue here that in a parallel way the variation in the form and style of textbooks might also be related to teacher coverage and gain. For teacher coverage the relationship is likely not in terms of what is covered (content) but in terms of how it is covered (pedagogy). The latter is likely related to learning. Even from the textbook point of view the structure and pedagogy of the book is likely to have an impact on a student's learning of the content intended by the book. At least this is our hypothesis –one that needs to be examined empirically.

In recent years a number of countries, perhaps most notably the US, have embarked on the formulation of policies intended to address perceived shortcomings of current educational delivery systems. A recurrent characteristic of these policy initiatives is that they proceed by bringing about changes in the content standards intended for the system, and subsequently involve a number of other policy instruments in reference to these standards. Policies regarding goals are often conceived of as joint mechanisms of system control or "system management" in conjunction with assessment systems [2] in which measurement procedures (most frequently achievement tests) and purposes (content standards) are held to provide a technically valid, and politically sufficient, system of governance.

Primacy in these governance systems is typically assigned to the policy instruments that set forth curricular intentions. A considerable body of work has been contributed to support the use of this type of governance in what has been termed content-driven systemic reform.[3] It is stated that ambitious curricula must be formulated and then appropriate mechanisms must be designed to implement these curricula so that students may have the opportunity to attain high levels of achievement. Content-based reform holds that a core set of policies regarding curriculum intentions provides a basis for determining which resources are necessary to ensure that students are provided the opportunities required to master curricular goals. Thus, the curriculum is intended to directly impact teacher training and certification, school course offerings, instructional resources, and systems of accountability.

Curriculum reform policy as presented in the reform theories reviewed above, assigns to standards documents, curriculum guides, frameworks, programs of study, and the like a primary role in defining potential educational experiences. They are intended to help shape goals and expectations for learning. These visions are presumed to guide the experiences of school children and are themselves important features of educational systems.

High expectations concerning the role of policies regarding curriculum intentions have certainly been held in most TIMSS countries. The majority reported a number of reforms and managed changes in the content, pedagogy, and technology prescribed in national curriculum policy for school mathematics and science. Of a total of 36 nations surveyed for this purpose during development of the TIMSS in the early 1990s, 29 nations reported such curricular reforms recently finished or underway in school mathematics and 28 nations did so in the case of school science.[4]

However, what is true of implementation? Current reform theory provides little guidance on the array of instruments essential to successful enactment of the various reformed visions of mathematics and science education. In this book we attempt to characterize one such possible instrument – the textbook. We argue that teachers and students (and the public) have always seen the textbook as a source of implementation criteria. It is likely that it is especially crucial in periods of reform as a source of such criteria. Findings from TIMSS suggest that textbooks are critical to the success of such endeavors. In work reported separately, we demonstrate how curriculum standards are statistically related to teacher implementation and to learning in TIMSS countries. However, in most cases this relationship is strongest when mediated through textbooks.[5] This makes it clear that textbooks are truly fulcrums whereby system-wide goals are likely to accomplish intended changes.

All of the countries in TIMSS that reported embarking upon reform or change in school mathematics or science stated that increased expectations regarding student performances with subject matter were at the core of those reforms. In many the new goals included problem solving, reasoning and communication – behaviors that had previously been less important in the mathematics or science curriculum. Unfortunately, we have seen here that the textbooks from TIMSS countries are often poor exemplars of such a vision. New subject matters may enter textbooks swiftly but new ways of exploring subject matter in classrooms were largely absent. It is no doubt to be expected that current policies for educational change start out with documenting bold new visions of school mathematics and science. However, it is disquieting that the primary relationship between system-wide policies and the achievement of children is through textbooks. Clearly textbook embodiments of bold new visions in the TIMSS study were very rare.

This brings to the fore the importance of the textbook as a mediator between policy and pedagogy. When challenged to change current and often long-held practices, teachers and students require compelling and valid examples of ways to meet these challenges. In some educational systems poor exemplification of goals in textbooks may be compensated for by strength in other instruments, for example, perhaps in examination systems or teacher training curricula. However, in contexts in which the overall governance of curriculum is weak, the absence of solid guidance from textbooks must amplify their negative influence on pedagogical practice. A good example of the latter may be the US and each of its individual states where no effective institutional mechanism exists to align instruments of curriculum policy. The existence of encyclopedic texts, with far more topics and far more episodic disjointed themes than those of most other textbooks in the TIMSS world, is likely to amplify the effects of the overall incoherence and lack of demand of these same books.

As efforts to explain cross-national differences in educational achievement progress, and as - more significantly – national efforts to enhance educational opportunities and student achievement continue, it is important to reflect on the meaning of the variation in educational experiences undergone by students in different educational systems. Elsewhere we characterized such variation in content coverage. Here we have characterized variation in form and style, which we believe can either help or hinder the learning of the content. Both are part of a textbook and as such textbooks and other instruments intended to bridge the gap between policy and practice are crucial to the enhancement of the quality of educational experiences undergone by students in class rooms, and by extention, equivalently crucial to the nature of their subsequent life chances.

Notes:

[1] In a separate volume (Schmidt et al. 2001) we present multivariate analyses specifying the relationship of textbook characteristics with instruction measured across the TIMSS nations.

[2] See Apple, 1990.

[3] See for example: Clune, 1993; O'Day & Smith, 1993.

[4] TIMSS participation questionnaire data reported previously (Schmidt, McKnight, Valverde, Houang, & Wiley, 1997b; Schmidt, Raizen, Britton, Bianchi, & Wolfe, 1997c).

[5] Schmidt et al. 2001.

REFERENCES

Alabama State Board of Education. 1999. *A message from the Alabama State Board of Education [to be pasted in all biology textbooks]* The Eagle Forum, 1995 [cited September 21 1999]. Available from http://www.eagleforum.org/educate/1995/dec95/textbook.html.

Aristotle. (1991). *On Rhetoric* (Kennedy, George A., Trans.). New York: Oxford University Press.

Ball, Deborah L., and Sharon Feiman - Nemser. 1988. Using textbooks and teacher's guides: A dilemma for beginning teachers and teacher educators. *Curriculum Inquiry* 18:401-423.

Barr, Rebecca, and Robert Dreeben. 1983. *How Schools Work*. Chicago: The University of Chicago Press.

Bidwell, Charles E., Kenneth A. Frank, and Pamela A. Quiroz. 1997. Teacher Types, Workplace Controls, and the Organization of Schools. *Sociology of Education* 70 (4):285-307.

Bidwell, Charles E., and John D. Kasarda. 1980. Conceptualizing and Measuring the Effects of School and Schooling. *American Journal of Education* 88 (4):401-430.

Bingham, Janet. 1998. Saxon math supporters cry charter. *Denver Post*, 5/9/98, B-01.

Brenton, M. 1982. Changing relationships in Dutch social services. *Journal of Social Policy* 11 (1):59-80.

Bridgeman, Anne, and Michael Fallon. 1985. California Rejects Science Texts and 'Watered-Down'. *Education Week*, 9/28.

Burstein, Leigh. 1993. Studying Learning, Growth, and Instruction Cross-Nationally: Lessons about why and why not engage in cross-national studies. In *The IEA Study of Mathematics III: Student Growth and Classroom Processes*, edited by L. Burstein. New York: Pergamon Press.

Burstein, Leigh, P. Aschbacher, Z. Chen, and Q. Sen. 1990. Establishing the Content Validity of Tests Designed To Serve Multiple Purposes: Bridging Secondary-Postsecondary Mathematics. Los Angeles: University of California Los Angeles, Center for Research on Evaluation, Standards, and Student Testing.

Chen, Jackie. 1997. The Textbook Revolution: Deciding What Children Learn. *Sinorama*, October.

Comber, L.C., and J.P Keeves. 1973. *Science Achievement in Seventeen Countries*. Stockholm: Almqvist and Wiksell.

Dreeben, Robert, and Rebecca Barr. 1988. Classroom Composition and the Design of Instruction. *Sociology of Education* 61 (3):129-142.

Dreeben, Robert, and Adam Gamoran. 1986. Race, Instruction, and Learning. *American Sociological Review* 51 (5):660-669.

Gamoran, Adam. 1987. The Stratification of High School Learning Opportunities. *Sociology of Education* 60:135-155.

Gamoran, Adam, and Matthew Weinstein. 1998. Differentiation and Opportunity in Restructured Schools. *American Journal of Education* 106 (3):385-415.

Guiton, Gretchen, and Jeannie Oakes. 1995. Opportunity to Learn and Conceptions of Educational Equality. *Educational Evaluation and Policy Analysis* 17 (3):323-336.

Hallinan, Maureen, and Aage B. Sorensen. 1977. *The Dynamics of Learning: A Conceptual Model.* Madison: Wisconsin University -Madison Institute for Research on Poverty.

Hallinan, Maureen T., and Aage B. Sorensen. 1983. The Formation and Stability of Instructional Groups. *American Sociological Review* 48 (6):838-851.

Hörner, W. 1981. The relationship between educational policy and educational research: the case of French curriculum reform. *European Journal of Science Education* 3 (2):217-221.

Kifer, Edward, Richard G. Wolfe, and William H. Schmidt. 1992. Understanding Patterns of Student Growth. In *The IEA Study of Mathematics III: Student Growth and Classroom Processes*, edited by L. Burstein. Oxford: Pergamon Press.

Kwong, Julia. 1988. Curriculum in Action: Mathematics in China's Elementary Schools. In *Textbooks in the Third World*, edited by P. G. Altbach and G. P. Kelly. New York: Garland Publishing, Inc.

Magnier, Andre. 1980. Changes in secondary school mathematical education in France over the last thirty years. In *Comparative Studies of Mathematics Curricula - Change and Stability 1960-1980*, edited by Institut fur Didaktik der Mathematik der Universitat Bielefeld. Bielefeld, Germany: Universitat Bielefeld.

McDonnell, Lorraine M. 1995. Opportunity to Learn as a Research Concept and a Policy Instrument. *Educational Evaluation and Policy Analysis* 17 (3):305-322.

McKnight, Curtis C. 1979. Model for the Second Study of Mathematics. In *Bulletin 4: Second IEA Study of Mathematics*. Urbana, Illinois: SIMS Study Center.

McKnight, Curtis C., and Gilbert A. Valverde. 1999. Explaining TIMSS Mathematics Achievement: A Preliminary Survey. In *International Comparisons in Mathematics Education*, edited by G. Kaiser, E. Luna and I. Huntley. London: Falmer Press.

Monk, David H. 1982. Resource Allocation in Classrooms: An Economic Analysis. *Journal of Curriculum Studies* 14 (2):167-181.

Monk, David H. 1984. Interdependencies among Educational Inputs and Resource Allocation in Classrooms. *Economics of Education Review.* 3 (1):65-73.

Monk, David H. 1996. Resource Allocation for Education: An Evolving and Promising Base for Policy-Oriented Research. *Journal of School Leadership* 6 (3):216-242.

Porter, Andrew C. 1991. Creating a System of School Process Indicators. *Educational Evaluation and Policy Analysis* 13:13-29.

Porter, Andrew C. 1993. School Delivery Standards. *Educational Researcher*, June-July, 24-30.

Resnick, Lauren B., Katherine J. Nolan, and Daniel P. Resnick. 1995. Benchmarking Education Standards. *Educational Evaluation and Policy Analysis* 17 (4):438-461.

Robitaille, David F., William H. Schmidt, Senta A. Raizen, Curtis C. McKnight, Edward D. Britton, and Cynthia Nicol. 1993. *Curriculum Frameworks for Mathematics and Science*. Edited by D. F. Robitaille. Vol. 1, *TIMSS Monograph Series*. Vancouver, Canada: Pacific Educational Press.

Roggie, Alyssa. 1997. Evolution "just a theory," district says. *Intelligencer Journal*, 7/19, A-1.

Schmidt, William H., and Leigh Burstein. 1992. Concomitants of Growth in Mathematics Achievement During the Population A School Year. In *The IEA Study of Mathematics III: Student Growth and Classroom Processes*, edited by L. Burstein. Oxford: Pergamon Press.

Schmidt, William H., and Leland Cogan. 1996. Development of the TIMSS Context Questionnaires. In *Technical Report. Volume 1: Design and Development*, edited by M. O. Martin and D. L. Kelly. Chestnut Hill, Massachusetts: Boston College.

Schmidt, William H., Doris Jorde, Leland Cogan, Emilie Barrier, Ignacio Gonzalo, Urs Moser, Katsuhiko Shimizu, Toshio Sawada, Gilbert A. Valverde, Curtis C. McKnight, Richard S. Prawat, David E. Wiley, Senta A. Raizen, Edward D. Britton, and Richard G. Wolfe. 1996. *Characterizing Pedagogical Flow: An Investigation of Mathematics and Science Teaching in Six Countries*. Dordrecht, The Netherlands: Kluwer Academic Publishers.

Schmidt, William H., and Curtis C. McKnight. 1995. Surveying Educational Opportunity in Mathematics and Science: An International Perspective. *Educational Evaluation and Policy Analysis* 17 (3):337-353.

Schmidt, William H., Curtis C. McKnight, Leland S. Cogan, Pamela M. Jakwerth, and Richard T. Houang. 1999. *Facing the Consequences: Using TIMSS for a Closer Look at U.S. Mathematics and Science Education*. Dordrecht, The Netherlands: Kluwer Academic Publishers.

Schmidt, William H., Curtis C. McKnight, Richard T. Houang, Hsing Chi Wang, David E. Wiley, Leland S. Cogan, and Richard G. Wolfe. 2001. *Why Schools Matter: Using TIMSS to Investigate Curriculum and Learning*. San Francisco: Jossey-Bass Publishers.

Schmidt, William H., Curtis C. McKnight, Senta A. Raizen, Pamela
     M. Jakwerth, Gilbert A. Valverde, Richard G. Wolfe, Edward
     D. Britton, Leonard J. Bianchi, and Richard T. Houang. 1997a.
     *A Splintered Vision: An Investigation of U.S. Science and
     Mathematics Education*. Dordrecht, The Netherlands: Kluwer
     Academic Publishers.

Schmidt, William H., Curtis C. McKnight, Gilbert A. Valverde, Richard
     T. Houang, and David E. Wiley. 1997b. *Many Visions, Many
     Aims: A Cross-National Investigation of Curricular Intentions in
     School Mathematics*. Vol. 1. Dordrecht, The Netherlands: Kluwer
     Academic Publishers.

Schmidt, William H., Andrew C. Porter, Robert C. Floden, Donald J.
     Freeman, and John R. Schwille. 1987. Four Patterns of Teacher
     Content Decision Making. *Journal of Curriculum Studies* 19
     (5):439-455.

Schmidt, William H., Senta A. Raizen, Edward D. Britton, Leonard J.
     Bianchi, and Richard G. Wolfe. 1997c. *Many Visions, Many Aims:
     A Cross-National Investigation of Curricular Intentions in School
     Science*. Vol. 2. Dordrecht, The Netherlands: Kluwer Academic
     Publishers.

Semrad, Staci. 1999. Math controversy adds up to debate. *Times Record
     News*, September 21.

Sosniak, Lauren, and Carole Perlman. 1990. Secondary Education by the
     Book. *Journal of Curriculum Studies* 22 (5):427-442.

Stevenson, David Lee, Kathryn S. Schiller, and Barbara Schneider. 1994.
     Sequences of Opportunities for Learning. *Sociology of Education*
     67 (3):184-198.

Survey of Mathematics and Science Opportunities. 1992a. *Document
     Analysis Manual*. East Lansing, MI: SMSO.

Survey of Mathematics and Science Opportunities. 1992b. *TIMSS Mathematics Curriculum Framework.* East Lansing, MI: SMSO.

Survey of Mathematics and Science Opportunities. 1992c. *TIMSS Science Curriculum Framework.* East Lansing, MI: SMSO.

Survey of Mathematics and Science Opportunities. 1992d. *Training Manual: Document Analysis, In-Depth Topic Trace Mapping Regional Training Meetings.* (77) East Lansing, MI: SMSO.

Survey of Mathematics and Science Opportunities. 1993a. *TIMSS Curriculum Analysis: A Content Analytic Approach.* East Lansing, MI: SMSO.

Survey of Mathematics and Science Opportunities. 1993b. *TIMSS: Concepts, Measurements, and Analyses.* East Lansing, MI: SMSO.

Thomas, J. Alan. 1977. Resource Allocation in Classrooms. Final Report. Washington D.C.: National Institute of Education, Project No. NIE-G-74-0037.

Thomas, J. Alan, and Frances Kemmerer. 1977. Money, Time and Learning. Final Report. Chicago: Spencer Foundation and National Institute of Education, Project No. 400-77-0094.

Valverde, Gilbert A. 1997. Evaluation and Curriculum Standards in an Era of Educational Reforms. In *Evaluation and Education Reform: Policy Options*, edited by B. Álvarez and M. Ruiz-Casares. Washington DC: U.S. Agency for International Development.

Valverde, Gilbert A., and William H. Schmidt. 2000. Greater Expectations: Learning from other nations in the quest for world-class standards in US school mathematics and science. *Journal of Curriculum Studies* 32 (5):651-687.

Appendix A
TIMSS CURRICULUM FRAMEWORKS:
MEASURING CURRICULAR ELEMENTS

The Third International Mathematics and Science Study (TIMSS) was designed to involve extensive data collections from participating national centers, an analysis of curriculum documents, a range of questionnaires, and complex attainment testing. This multi-component data collection (carried out in participating countries and at several international sites) made it essential that all TIMSS components be linked by a common category framework and descriptive language. Whether classifying a test item, characterizing part of a curriculum document, or linking a questionnaire item to other TIMSS parts, any description had to use common terms, categories, and standardized procedures to assign numerical codes for entry into the appropriate database.

This common language was provided by two framework documents – one for the sciences and one for mathematics. Each covered the full range of the years of schooling in a unified category system. Each framework was articulated first only in technical reports (as is still true for more extensive explanatory notes) but has now been reproduced and documented in a monograph.[1]

Each framework document was multi-faceted and multi-layered. It considered three aspects of subject matter content and performance – *content* (subject matter topic), *performance expectation* (what students were expected to do with particular content), and *perspective* (any over-arching orientation to the subject matter and its place among the disciplines and in the everyday world). Content as subject matter topic is relatively clear; "performance expectation" is less so. It was decided not to attempt identifying student (cognitive) performance processes – which would be highly inferential, particularly subject to cultural differences, and thus not feasible in a cross-cultural context. It was decided rather to specify expectations for student (science and mathematics) performances – for example, formulating or clarifying a problem to be solved, developing a solution strategy, verifying a problem solution, and so on, without positing cognitive means for producing the performances. This focused on more generic, less culture-bound task expectations and demands. Postulating specific cognitive processes necessarily would have involved culturally tied cognitive categories inherent in student thinking in any given country.

In addition to being a multi-aspect system, each framework was designed for using multiple categories. Each element – curriculum guide, textbook segment, test item –could be considered as part of more than one category of any framework aspect. Each element was to be classified in as many framework categories as needed to capture its richness. Each would have a unique, often complex "signature" – a set of content, performance expectation, and perspective categories that characterized it, at least in terms of the framework's three aspects. This system is flexible – allowing simple or more complex signatures as needed.

Such flexible multidimensionality was essential for analyzing curriculum documents. How often segments involved multiple contents or performance expectations had to be determined empirically by the documents, not by the study design. Characterizing mathematics and science curricula required a tool permitting coherent categorization of curriculum guides' and text-books' major pedagogical features. It had to be capable of translating many nationally idiosyncratic ways for specifying mathematics and science education goals into a common specification language. The TIMSS mathematics and science curriculum frameworks were designed to be such a tool.

Framework development was cross-national. The frameworks had to be suitable for all participating countries and educational systems. Representing the interests of many countries, the frameworks were designed cross-nationally and passed through several iterations. The result is imperfect, but it is still a step forward in cross-national comparisons of curricular documents. Its value may be judged by the results of this and related volumes.

Each framework aspect is organized hierarchically using nested subcategories of increasing specificity. Within a given level, the arrangement of topics does not reflect a particular rational ordering of the content. See Figure A.1 for an overview of the content aspect of the science framework. The end of this appendix briefly presents all three aspects of the mathematics and science frameworks. Each framework was meant to be encyclopedic – intended to cover all possibilities at some level of specificity. No claim is made that the "grain size" – the level of specificity for each aspect's categories – is the same throughout the framework. Some subcategories are more inclusive and commonly used, others less so. Specificity had broad commonalties but also considerable variation among the participating countries. This varying granularity requires special care in designing framework-based methods and interpreting the results of their use.

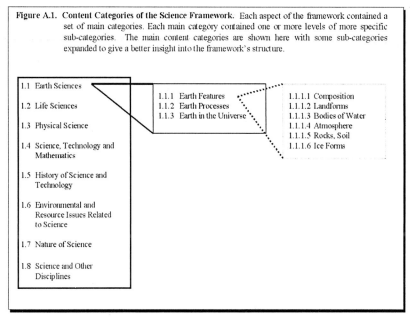

Figure A.1. Content Categories of the Science Framework. Each aspect of the framework contained a set of main categories. Each main category contained one or more levels of more specific sub-categories. The main content categories are shown here with some sub-categories expanded to give a better insight into the framework's structure.

In the mathematics framework, *content* involves 10 major categories, each with 2 to 17 subcategories. Some subcategories are divided still further. The level of detail and organization reflects a compromise between simplicity (fewer categories) and specificity (more categories). The hierarchical levels of increasing specificity allow some flexibility in detail level and generalization.

In the science framework, *content* involves eight major categories, each with two to six sub-categories. Some subcategories are divided further. The level of detail and organization reflects compromise between simplicity (fewer categories) and specificity (more categories). The hierarchical levels of increasing specificity allow some flexibility in detail level and generalization.

Performance expectations is a flexible category system (see below for details), but — as with the other framework aspects — no category or subcategory is considered exclusive. Any document segment should involve at least one or more performance expectation categories from the framework. Complex, integrated performances can thus be characterized in detail — as can contents and perspectives. This differs from traditional grid classifications that generate unique categorizations combining one element from two or more dimensions.

Complex signatures reveal important differences in how curricula are meant to achieve their goals. They show differences in how subject matter elements are combined — and differences in what students are expected to do. Each framework can reveal subject matter presented in an integrated, thematic way, with a rich set of performance expectations for students as recommended by curriculum reformers in many countries. However, it also allows simpler "signatures" – for example, those often associated with more traditional curricula and many traditional achievement test items.

What follows is a listing of the content, performance expectation, and perspective codes of the mathematics framework. For a more detailed discussion, see the book referenced in footnote 1 of this appendix or the technical report of "Explanatory Notes" for the mathematics framework.

Content

1.1 Numbers
   1.1.1   Whole numbers
           1.1.1.1   Meaning
           1.1.1.2   Operations
           1.1.1.3   Properties of operations
   1.1.2   Fractions and decimals
           1.1.2.1   Common fractions
           1.1.2.2   Decimal fractions
           1.1.2.3   Relationships of common and decimal fractions
           1.1.2.4   Percentages
           1.1.2.5   Properties of common and decimal fractions
   1.1.3   Integer, rational, and real numbers
           1.1.3.1   Negative numbers, integers, and their properties
           1.1.3.2   Rational numbers and their properties
           1.1.3.3   Real numbers, their subsets, and their properties
   1.1.4   Other numbers and number concepts
           1.1.4.1   Binary arithmetic and/or other number bases
           1.1.4.2   Exponents, roots, and radicals
           1.1.4.3   Complex numbers and their properties
           1.1.4.4   Number theory

1.9   Validation and structure
   1.9.1   Validation and justification
   1.9.2   Structuring and abstracting

1.10 Other content
   1.10.1 Informatics

Performance Expectations
2.1   Knowing
   2.1.1   Representing
   2.1.2   Recognizing equivalents
   2.1.3   Recalling mathematical objects and properties

2.2   Using routine procedures
   2.2.1   Using equipment
   2.2.2   Performing routine procedures
   2.2.3   Using more complex procedures

2.3   Investigating and problem solving
   2.3.1   Formulating and clarifying problems and situations
   2.3.2   Developing strategy
   2.3.3   Solving
   2.3.4   Predicting
   2.3.5   Verifying

2.4   Mathematical reasoning
   2.4.1   Developing notation and vocabulary
   2.4.2   Developing algorithms
   2.4.3   Generalizing
   2.4.4   Conjecturing
   2.4.5   Justifying and proving
   2.4.6   Axiomatizing

2.5   Communicating
   2.5.1   Using vocabulary and notation
   2.5.2   Relating representations
   2.5.3   Describing/discussing
   2.5.4   Critiquing

Perspectives
3.1   Attitudes toward science, mathematics, and technology

3.2   Careers involving science, mathematics and technology
    3.2.1   Promoting careers in science, mathematics, and technology
    3.2.2   Promoting the importance of science, mathematics, and
           technology in nontechnical careers

3.3   Participation in science and mathematics by underrepresented
groups

3.4   Science, mathematics, and technology to increase interest

3.5   Scientific and mathematical habits of mind

The following is a brief listing of the content, performance expectation, and
perspective codes of the science framework. For a more detailed discussion
see the monograph referenced or the technical report of "Explanatory
Notes" for the science framework.

1.1   Earth sciences
    1.1.1   Earth features
           1.1.1.1   Composition
           1.1.1.2   Landforms
           1.1.1.3   Bodies of water
           1.1.1.4   Atmosphere
           1.1.1.5   Rocks, soil
           1.1.1.6   Ice forms
    1.1.2   Earth processes
           1.1.2.1   Weather and climate
           1.1.2.2   Physical cycles
           1.1.2.3   Building and breaking
           1.1.2.4   Earth's history
    1.1.3   Earth in the universe
           1.1.3.1   Earth in the solar system
           1.1.3.2   Planets in the solar system
           1.1.3.3   Beyond the solar system
           1.1.3.4   Evolution of the universe

1.2   Life sciences
  1.2.1   Diversity, organization, structure of living things
      1.2.1.1   Plants, fungi
      1.2.1.2   Animals
      1.2.1.3   Other organisms
      1.2.1.4   Organs, tissues
      1.2.1.5   Cells
  1.2.2   Life processes and systems enabling life functions
      1.2.2.1   Energy handling
      1.2.2.2   Sensing and responding
      1.2.2.3   Biochemical processes in cells
  1.2.3   Life spirals, genetic continuity, diversity
      1.2.3.1   Life cycles
      1.2.3.2   Reproduction
      1.2.3.3   Variation and inheritance
      1.2.3.4   Evolution, speciation, diversity
      1.2.3.5   Biochemistry of genetics
  1.2.4   Interactions of living things
      1.2.4.1   Biomes and ecosystems
      1.2.4.2   Habitats and niches
      1.2.4.3   Interdependence of life
      1.2.4.4   Animal behavior
  1.2.5   Human biology and health
      1.2.5.1   Nutrition
      1.2.5.2   Disease

1.3   Physical sciences
  1.3.1   Matter
      1.3.1.1   Classification of matter
      1.3.1.2   Physical properties
      1.3.1.3   Chemical properties
  1.3.2   Structure of matter
      1.3.2.1   Atoms, ions, molecules
      1.3.2.2   Macromolecules, crystals
      1.3.2.3   Subatomic particles
  1.3.3   Energy and physical processes
      1.3.3.1   Energy types, sources, conversions
      1.3.3.2   Heat and temperature
      1.3.3.3   Wave phenomena

1.6.6   Effects of natural disasters

1.7   Nature of science
    1.7.1   Nature of scientific knowledge
    1.7.2   The scientific enterprise

1.8   Science and other disciplines
    1.8.1   Science and mathematics
    1.8.2   Science and other disciplines

Performance expectations
2.1   Understanding
    2.1.1   Simple information
    2.1.2   Complex information
    2.1.3   Thematic information

2.2   Theorizing, analyzing, and solving problems
    2.2.1   Abstracting and deducing scientific principles
    2.2.2   Applying scientific principles to solve quantitative problems
    2.2.3   Applying scientific principles to develop explanations
    2.2.4   Constructing, interpreting, and applying models
    2.2.5   Making decisions

2.3   Using tools, routine procedures, and science processes
    2.3.1   Using apparatus, equipment, and computers
    2.3.2   Conducting routine experimental operations
    2.3.3   Gathering data
    2.3.4   Organizing and representing data
    2.3.5   Interpreting data

2.4   Investigating the natural world
    2.4.1   Identifying questions to investigate
    2.4.2   Designing investigations
    2.4.3   Conducting investigations
    2.4.4   Interpreting investigational data
    2.4.5   Formulating conclusions from investigational data

2.5   Communicating
    2.5.1   Accessing and processing information
    2.5.2   Sharing information

Perspectives
3.1   Attitudes towards science, mathematics, and technology
    3.1.1   Positive attitudes toward science, mathematics, and technology
    3.1.2   Skeptical attitudes towards use of science and technology

3.2   Careers in science, mathematics and technology
    3.2.1   Promoting careers in science, mathematics, and technology
    3.2.2   Promoting importance of science, mathematics, and technology in non-technical careers

3.3   Participation in science and mathematics by underrepresented groups

3.4   Science, mathematics, and technology to increase interest

3.5   Safety in science performance

3.6   Scientific habits of mind

Notes:

[1] Robitaille, D. F. and others, Curriculum Frameworks for Mathematics and Science, (Vancouver: Pacific Educational Press, 1993).

Appendix B
LIST OF EXHIBITS:

Chapter 1

Chapter 2

Chapter 4

Chapter 5

The Authors

Gilbert A. Valverde received his undergraduate degree in Philosophy at the Universidad de Costa Rica, and his Ph.D. in Administrative, Institutional and Policy Studies from the Comparative Education Center at The University of Chicago. Currently he is on the faculty of the Comparative and International Educational Policy Program at the University at Albany, State University of New York. He specializes in the cross-national study of curriculum policies, focusing on the role of educational standards, indicator systems, textbook and assessment policy in the configuration of educational opportunity structures. In addition to his ongoing work with the US National Research Center (where he was Senior Researcher and Associate Director from 1992 until 1998), he is also conducting research on curriculum governance in the context of education reforms underway in Latin America. Both lines of research inquire into the role of curriculum governance in the configuration of the social, political, and pedagogical conditions that provide pupils opportunities to acquire knowledge, to develop skills, and to form attitudes concerning school subjects. Dr. Valverde is a member of the Working Group on Standards and Evaluation of the Program to Promote Educational Reform in Latin America (PREAL). He has also served as advisor or consultant on standards, curriculum governance, and educational indicators policies to the World Bank, NASA, the Inter-American Development Bank, and the US Agency for International Development – and to a number of ministries, foundations, school districts, non-governmental organizations, and special interest groups in the Americas.

Leonard J. Bianchi received his undergraduate degree in psychology from Case-Western Reserve and his Ph.D. in Measurement and Quantitative Methods at Michigan State University. He is currently Director of the Research and Evaluation Department for the Flint Community School System. He spent three years in New Zealand as the director of the Data Processing Center for the IEA Second International Mathematics Study and five years with the US National Research Center for the TIMSS as a senior researcher. He has consulted with the World Bank on analysis of the IEA Second International Science Study (SISS). He has worked on educational policy at both the national and local level. His expertise lies in both statistical analysis and psychometrics. Dr. Bianchi has also worked in medical certification with the American Board of Emergency Medicine.

Richard G. Wolfe is an Associate Professor at the Ontario Institute for Studies in Education of the University of Toronto, Department of Curriculum, Teaching, and Learning Measurement and Evaluation program), Toronto, Ontario, Canada. He was the consultant on methodology to the international mathematics committee for the IEA Second International Mathematics Study (SIMS), prepared the databank for the IEA Second International Science Study (SISS), and contributed to the analysis and reporting for both studies. He was the chairman of the sampling and methodology committee for the Third International Mathematics and Science Study (TIMSS) during its initial design stages. He has worked with a number of state assessment programs and with national and international assessment projects in Latin America. His specialties are assessment survey design, sampling, and data analysis.

William H. Schmidt received his undergraduate degree in mathematics from Concordia College in River Forrest, IL and his Ph.D. from the University of Chicago in psychometrics and applied statistics. He carries the title of University Distinguished Professor at Michigan State University and the National Research Coordinator and Executive Director of the US National Center which oversees participation of the United States in the IEA sponsored Third International Mathematics and Science Study (TIMSS). He was also a member of the Senior Executive staff and Head of the Office of Policy Studies and Program Assessment for the National Science Foundation in Washington, DC from1986-1988. He is widely published in numerous journals including the Journal of the American Statistical Association, Journal of Educational Statistics, Multivariate Behavioral Research, Journal of Education Psychology, Journal of Educational Measurement, Educational and Psychological Measurement Journal, American Educational Research Journal and the Journal of Curriculum Studies and has delivered numerous papers at conferences including the American Educational Research Association, Psychometric Society, American Sociological Association, International Reading Association and National Council of Teachers of Mathematics. He has also co-authored seven books related to the Third International Mathematics and Science Study.   He was awarded the Honorary Doctorate Degree at Concordia University in 1997 and most recently received the 1998 Willard Jacobson Lectureship from the New York Academy of Sciences.

Richard T. Houang earned his Ph.D. in Educational Psychology with specialization in Psychometrics and statistical methods from the University of California at Santa Barbara. He joined the faculty at Michigan State University in 1979 and has taught courses in research designs and multivariate analysis. He has worked with the US TIMSS National Research Center since 1994 and is currently the Associate Director. He is currently a member of the Telecommunications Committee for the American Education Research Associations. Dr. Houang has published in numerous journals including American Educational Research Journal, Educational Studies in Mathematics, and Perceptual and Motor Skills and has delivered numerous papers at conferences including the American Educational Research Association. He has also co-authored several books related to the Third International Mathematics and Science Study.